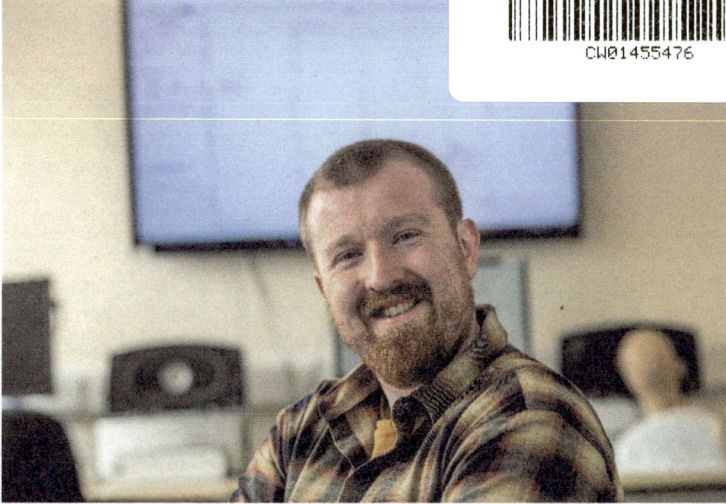

About the Author

Barnaby Growling can only be described as an unorthodox triple threat: Poet, Audiologist and Author in that order. At the tender age of eleven, he was selected by the UK Young Writers initiative for publication in the poetry anthology Hidden Treasures Bristol: Volume 1. Eventually, expanding into prose, Barnaby proved quite the unlikeable show-off; by winning both the Jos Millar Prize from the British Society of Audiology, and the D W Robinson Prize from the Institute of Acoustics in successive years. He now resides in Queensland Australia, where nobody knows nor cares about any of this, and quite right too!

Confessions of an Australian Assimilator

Barnaby Growling

Confessions of an Australian Assimilator

Olympia Publishers
London

www.olympiapublishers.com
OLYMPIA PAPERBACK EDITION

A CIP catalogue record for this title is
available from the British Library.

ISBN: 978-1-80439-265-2

This is a work of fiction.
Names, characters, places and incidents originate from the writer's
imagination. Any resemblance to actual persons, living or dead, is
purely coincidental.

First Published in 2023

Olympia Publishers
Tallis House
2 Tallis Street
London
EC4Y 0AB

Printed in Great Britain

Dedication

Firstly, I dedicate this book to my family and closest friends. You know who you are, and although you couldn't be with me in person, I carried you with me every step of the way. Lastly, I dedicate this book to the citizens of Australia; you were my muse and this book would be nothing without you.

Acknowledgements

Thank you to my Dad, Julian Davis and to my friend, Connor Grotzke. You both took nothing but interest in my hopeful endeavours, and proofread the manuscript for this book. Thank you to Tracy and Marty. You both helped to fact-check the accuracy of my recollections, and never once questioned the likelihood of my success out loud.

I

ARE YOU CRAZY OR JUST PLAIN STUPID?

A valid question. My answer benefits from some historical context, because it's an understatement to say that the prospect of immigrating to Australia was a different kettle of fish back in 2019. I should explain. On the day that I formally submitted my very first expression of interest for securing employment in Australia, on the 7th of March 2019, I was twenty-seven years old. By that point in my life I had already spent five years at university to qualify as an Audiologist, toting undergraduate and postgraduate qualifications by the end of my sentence, which was subsequently complimented by over three years of post-graduate experience working in the National Health Service (NHS). Unlike many of my peers, I had avoided the powerful clutches of post-university debt for the most part, because the tuition fees for my four-year Bachelor of Science (BSc) had been funded by the government; in their attempt to bolster the shortfall in Audiologists required to meet the hearing loss demands of an aging British population. I lived at home for just over two years, after I graduated from my BSc, so that I could save most of my full-time salary to fund a Master of Science (MSc).

It felt wise to obtain a master's degree at the time; to serve as an investment for anticipated career advancement either at home or abroad potentially. Commonwealth countries like: Australia, Canada, and New Zealand do not accept overseas qualified Audiologists to their shores if they don't have a MSc. Considering the economic uncertainties surrounding Brexit at that time, leaving UK shores for a prosperous life abroad was quite a palatable option. So, not only was I: healthy, suitably qualified, able-bodied, crimeless, and debtless, I was also unmarried and childless which meant that I had no legally binding dependents anchoring me to blighty. It seemed to me that if there was ever a year to gamble on an international adventure with the promise of: broader training opportunities, transnational work experience, and salaries which typically amounted to double my UK earnings, it was 2019. Back then, a twentysomething pom travelling out to work in Australia didn't seem so far out of reach, but a lot can happen in two years.

II

MORRISON'S PREFERRED M-WORD

By 2019, Australia's appetite for skilled migration had changed; city dwellers were now feeling the pinch of overpopulation and rural Aussies were still feeling the pinch of underpopulation. The Turnbull Government's replacement of the 457 VISA program, on the 18th of March 2018, with the significantly more discriminatory 482 VISA program signified the beginning of a new breed of 'Australia First' politics. The 457 VISA program was installed by the Howard Government, in 1996, and reached its peak in 2013 where 126,348 VISA's were granted, compared to only 25,786 in the programs first year. Back in the 457 days, 650 skilled jobs were on the eligibility list and the VISA itself was open ended. This meant that all 457 VISA holders were guaranteed four years in Australia, and this meant they could all apply for permanent residency at the end of their term, if they so wished. Furthermore, the 457 program permitted employers to make use of fast-track sponsorship arrangements, so that they could get hold of international talent more quickly. According to ABC news, the top three countries making the most of what the 457 VISA program had to offer were: India (where over twenty-five per cent of successful applicants came from), the UK (where 19.5 per cent of successful applicants came from), and China (where 5.8 per cent of successful applicants came from).

Nonetheless, in response to announcements from the Turnbull Government that the 457 VISA program would be abolished in 2017, the number of 457 VISA applications that were granted that year, fell by 35.7 per cent in three months. When it came in, the 482 VISA program sought to axe 216 skilled jobs from the government's eligibility list, and it made it more expensive for both sponsors and applicants to apply for. Employers now had to work harder to prove that there was a demand for jobs, which could not be filled by an Australian, by conducting labour market testing. Even if the employer succeeded in this task, they were then stung by the additional cost of a new training levy, which had to be paid annually for the entire length of the skilled applicants VISA; as a penalty for electing not to hire an Australian. English language requirements for non-native speakers were also tightened, and not all 482 VISA applicants were guaranteed four years in Australia. Some only got two years depending on their job role, which meant that they could not apply for permanent residency at the end of their term. In other words, Australia's philosophy towards skilled migrants had reversed from *'if you've got it we want it' to 'take nothing but photographs leave nothing but footprints, got it?'*

By the time I started applying for jobs in Australia, the 482 VISA program had been in full swing for twelve months. Nevertheless, this time elapse didn't seem to stop my prospective employers, who had been slowly weaned from the more accommodating 457 VISA program, from stepping on mines in the shape of 482 processing fees and administrative heft. My very first Australian job application in March 2019 was actually successful, which confirmed my then naïve doctrine that Australia definitely needed, and, more to the point, wanted foreign workers. But the job offer fell through several weeks later, during the VISA application process, because once the substantial cost of the 482 VISA application became concrete to my employer, they did not hesitate to inform me that bringing me on board was no longer commercially viable, and *'sorry for the inconvenience'.* That first disappointment was where I began to realise that getting to Australia might not be as straightforward as I thought. It turned out that even if you got offered a job, and subsequently signed an employment contract, it all meant nothing without a VISA. A migrant with a job offer in another country, without a VISA, is a man who owns a car with no petrol, it symbolises freedom and adventure, but right now he's going nowhere.

As the mounting obstacles surrounding the 482 VISA program raised their heads above the parapet, I decided to seek the help of a healthcare recruitment agency. They would have dealt with applicants like me numerous times, I thought, and would almost certainly have had dealings with Australian employers in rural communities; where the demand for skilled labour was highest. I concluded that my chances were highest with them, because rural employers would likely have no choice but to pay the 482 VISA fees and penalties, just to keep their businesses alive. My instincts were right on that one, and I was put in touch with an Audiology clinic owner in rural New South Wales (NSW), in June 2019. She informed me that although she was in need of a skilled migrant due to a lack of interest from Australian Audiologists, most of whom were happy in Sydney, to invite sponsorship she would need: *"to have enough information to clearly validate a case, and I will be exploring some areas quite deeply to try and achieve this"*. She was true to her word.

Here are some of the highlights. The first skype interview was two hours thirty-eight minutes and forty-four seconds. The second skype interview was thirteen days later, and lasted two hours ten minutes and twenty-three seconds. Both broke personal records for the longest interviews I had ever been a part of. I was then required to provide a full list of references to vouch for *every* prior work and academic position that I had ever held (six in total). Furthermore, each of the nominated referees, who had provided a reference for me, were themselves interviewed for thirty minutes apiece. I was informed later that they were asked to answer questions about what it was like to work with me. Just so you know, to work as an Audiologist in Australia, you need to become a member of Audiology Australia (AA). There are three stages to this process. In short, Stage 1 requires the submission of an extensive range of independently certified documents; to prove your credentials as a qualified overseas Audiologist. For me, this involved booking an appointment with my local Pharmacist to get copies of both my BSc, and MSc, degree certificates and transcripts signed and stamped. It also involved scanning over a hundred pages worth of my original BSc placement logbooks, and course curriculum handbooks, for AA's consideration.

Stage 2 of the AA registration process involves passing their nasty little overseas written exam. The exam is a 3 ½ hour MSc level assessment, composing six case studies designed to test the breadth and depth of your clinical knowledge across multiple audiological specialisms. It is only held twice a year. Furthermore, it was not possible for me to sit the exam in the UK. This meant that I had to fly seventeen hours to the University of Western Australia to sit it. I sat the exam on the 2/10/19 and received my results just over eight weeks later. The AA later informed me that only twenty per cent of candidates passed the exam that I took that year. This is actually an improvement; in 2012 the pass rate was only 12.5per cent. I was finally offered the job as a senior audiologist on the 16th of December 2019 but, after all of this, with a job offer and no VISA I was once again the owner of a shiny new car with no petrol. Furthermore, circumstances were about to become heavily complicated by the fact that the land down under was about to catch fire.

III

TRIAPHILIA: BAD THINGS HAPPEN IN THREE'S

The now infamous Black Summer was far from normal. It set Australia ablaze between September 2019 and March 2020, where it scorched an almost continuous 1,160 km strip from south east Queensland to eastern Victoria, encompassing 7.04 million hectares of land, of which 5.7 million hectares of forest and woodland was burnt, devastating Australian communities and killing and injuring an estimated three billion animals. It's estimated over 2,500 homes were destroyed and the fires directly caused thirty-three human deaths, and almost four hundred and fifty more from smoke inhalation. Suffice to say that even though Prime Minister Scott Morrison infamously went on holiday to Hawaii, during Black Summer, the Australian Government were heavily preoccupied during this time. Unfortunately for me, this also happened to be the time when my 482 VISA nomination was being processed, along with all the documentation that my new employer had submitted to prove my legitimacy in filling the role. My VISA nomination application was sent in by my employer on the 18/12/19. As desperate as I was to get to Australia by that time after such an exhausting selection process, I couldn't rightfully blame the Australian Government for me not being very high on their priority list, while their homeland was burning around them. Looking back on it now, Black Summer's effect on my prospects of getting to Australia, in isolation, would probably have been relatively minimal. Little did I know at the time, but the delays that I selfishly cursed Black Summer for inflicting upon me would be nothing compared to the globally disruptive force that was lurking around the corner, in Wuhan Province.

SARS-CoV-2 changed everything. Australia closed its borders to all non-citizens and non-residents on Friday the 20th of March 2020. UK Prime Minister Boris Johnson announced the first COVID 19 lockdown in the UK on the 23rd of March respectively. I was considered an essential worker for the NHS during this period so I was lucky enough not to permanently lose my job, and become dependent on furlough. I can very distinctly recall how everything was surreally business as usual, on the streets of Britain, on the lead up to the lockdown. I was encountering patients at work who were attending their appointments with me after casually returning from holidays in hotspots like Italy and Greece, who openly declared: *'yeah I have been feeling a bit off ever since I came back from holiday actually. I'm a bit sinus anyway with flying but now it's like one of those colds that won't go away you know'*.

The first official case of COVID 19 was recorded in my home county of South Gloucestershire on the 11th of March. Considering my close proximity to the vectors merrily returning from the Mediterranean at the time, I shouldn't really have been surprised when I was conscripted by the universe to become one of the first to contract the virus. My instinctive diagnostic suspicions were not objectively confirmed until the 13th of July, when I eventually managed to receive a laboratory-based antibody test at my nearest hospital, which at that time were not universally received or readily available.

I was temporarily released from my duties and told to stay

home by my line managers on the 29th of March. I became significantly symptomatic soon after. The moment I realised that something wasn't right was when one sunny afternoon I was barely able to finish cutting the lawn, due to what can only be described as unearned heavyweight exhaustion. My get up and go had got up and went. For the next three days following I was served an acute dressing of COVID 19 malaise on a base of: draining fatigue, compound muscular aches, lack of appetite, hot and cold flushes, compromised taste, fleeting tinnitus, and restricted breathing with a side of impending doom and vertigo.

The vertigo was especially annoying because it would always seem to hit me at the most inopportune moments, such as when I was holding tomato soup in my hand, or when I was relieving myself in the lavatory. One especially sobering attack, on the evening of the 2nd day, rendered me temporarily blind for an estimate of ten-twenty seconds. Gratefully, my vision shimmered back into view; gifting me the confidence to re-release my pelvic floor muscles to enjoy the sweet relief of finishing what I had started moments earlier. COVID 19 was an especially uneasy sickness for me because I was hosting a prototype pathogen that humanity didn't properly understand. The virus of March 2020 had proved to be lethal to not just the elderly, but even the fittest amongst us in the form of Olympic athletes. Was it Bats? Was it Pangolins? Nobody seemed to know. Spoiler alert; I pulled through, and I count myself lucky that I was not consciously left with any permanent weaknesses secondary to long COVID. My time with the virus was gone almost as fast as it had come.

There was a silver lining which emerged from my time spent hosting the microscopic devil from Wuhan; I am an original cohort member of the Avon Longitudinal Study of Parents and

Aging (ALSPAC) which is also known as Children of the 90's. Their pioneering research dutifully continued throughout the lockdown and when they heard of my confirmed COVID antibodies, in July 2020, I was dutifully invited to their research centre in Clifton to give blood samples which were later used to aid in the development of the original Oxford AstraZeneca vaccine.

As the pandemic endured, and the UK began to realise that it wouldn't all be *'over by Christmas'* so to speak, I eventually returned to work in the juggernaut that is Southmead Hospital. I was now covered head to toe in Personal Protective Equipment (PPE), while I waited for news of my VISA nomination. All the while trying not to get disproportionately frustrated at my: friends, family, and work colleague's greatest hits: *"Any news yet?" "Nothing yet". When are you off then?" "I'm not sure".* Radio silence endured until the 9/7/2020, where I finally got the email that took me off my tenterhooks; I had been deemed worthy and my VISA nomination had been approved. Taken at face value, this would seem like purely good news and it did mean that I had something positive to share with interested parties, when they inevitably enquired about my progress. Nonetheless, securing the nomination came to feel like one step forwards and two steps back, because I was now facing a conundrum.

IV

THIS IS AUSTRALIA CALLING

On the 9th of July 2020, VISA nomination in hand, I found myself at a fork in the road. To express the full gravity of my dilemma, I have included the actual deliberations that I had with my employer in Australia, via email, at this juncture so that you can appreciate all the balls with which we were juggling.

9/7/20

Australia: I'm delighted to tell you that your visa nomination is approved. I'm saddened to tell you that until the national borders open, that, as I understand it, you are unable to enter Australia. That is unless you have compassionate grounds to gain an exception or take a shot at the critical skill shortage avenue. Our profession is regarded medical and essential. You would need a two-week quarantine on arrival. I've been spending some time looking into this and will continue to do so. Recently we had an outbreak in Melbourne and our state borders have closed with Victoria and our Southern friends are in lockdown again.

Me: Here is my situation at the present time. The UK is slowly easing the lockdown restrictions; people are allowed to be within one metre of each other now, but just like Melbourne, we have also been struggling with local outbreaks. The city of Leicester had to remain in a more secure lockdown due to a sudden outbreak. At present, I am timetabled to see patients up until the 30th of July. Going forward from there, appointments will be booked on an ad hoc basis depending on what the hospital needs. I have had a look at the Australian government immigration website, and I can see what you mean. Now that I have the nomination, I tried out the exemption travel request form to see what it would entail and I don't want to sound defeatist after coming so far, but I am not sure whether we would have much success with it. Despite the fact that I have been categorised as having critical skills that Australia wants, there is a section which asks: *'Please explain why you need to travel to Australia now'*. I am not sure whether I have what would be judged as a truly compelling reason other than, *'This has been a long time coming and I really want to get started as soon as possible please'*. Which I doubt will suffice.

Furthermore, it looks like they can take a while to make a decision, based on their advice not to have travel plans booked earlier than four weeks, from the time you put in your application. If my responsibilities in the UK take me to the end of July anyway, it seems like there could be a toss-up between whether we take on the stress of applying for the exemption, and see where that leads over the coming weeks, or we wait and see whether the Australian government eases the national travel ban, and go from there. Also, it seems like they want details of the booked flight itinerary as part of the application, which seems like a fair risk to book at the moment, particularly with a travel ban in place and no guarantee of refunds.

If you think it's worth putting the work in to submit the application, then I will work alongside you to do it, but I also understand if you think it's more suitable to wait and see if the travel ban eases; which might make our lives significantly easier in the process all things considered.

15/7/20

Australia: things are changing rapidly here as a second wave is breaking loose. Flights into Australia have been reduced and lock down imposed on several regional areas.

As you suggest I'd like to hold off for a moment and review our situation again in September. Thank you for your patience

3/10/20

Me: My impending fear is that if this travel ban continues into next year and beyond, then the VISA nomination that we have worked so hard to obtain will expire. I noticed on the paperwork that it comes with a disclaimer, saying that if you do not act on the nomination within twelve months then it will expire. That by my calculations gives us until June of 2021.

4/10/20

Australia: The good news is that Australian cases have come back under control again. A few states (Victoria) must prove longevity and I think twenty days is the time frame. Internal Borders (some) are looking to be re-opened and international travel bubbles opened up. International arrivals have increased by fifty per cent to six thousand per month. Things are beginning to move. We can apply for an exemption and I'm happy to support you here. The thing that is difficult to obtain at reasonable cost and reliability - at this stage, is a flight. I'm optimistic but realistic. We are just coming out of a heavy lockdown in Victoria. There is a bit more info on the web site so do check it out.

5/10/20

Me: I have had a look at all of the information available on the Australian Government website. First of all, before I can go ahead and fill in the exemption form, I need my VISA to be processed and certified. Currently, I only have a VISA nomination. Up until now, the Immigration Department has advised that candidates should not apply for a VISA due to the COVID travel restrictions. But if we are going ahead with applying for the travel exemption I will need an approved VISA to complete the form.

Would you like me to go ahead and apply for the VISA?

14/10/20

Australia: There are a few balls in the air and out of our reach in terms of information, much less control. There are also approx. thirty thousand Australians awaiting allocated flights and associated quarantine to come home. I believe the quota is six thousand per month. There is a lot of political pressure to increase the quota, but at the moment that's where it is. Given the waiting times for Visas, yes, go ahead, you will require it anyway.

Me: Okay, VISA application it is then. I will get the ball rolling on that one ASAP and let you know how things go. I was keeping my nomination in the chamber just in case my application got denied for COVID 19 related reasons, causing us to have to start again. But, as you say, without it we can't complete the travel exemption form.

So, that is what I did. With a deep breath, and an unnatural number of paranoia checks, I took the plunge and formally submitting my VISA application on Saturday the 24th of October 2020 at 8:30pm. Why the delay? I hear you ask. I implore you to forgive me for being slightly jittery at this point in proceedings, because it felt like I only had one shot at this, and the VISA application process itself was no mean feat. The online application form had twenty-two separate parts to complete, each of which required supporting documentation as evidence for my written answers. By the time I was finished, I had attached twenty-eight different documents to my application, which in addition to my VISA nomination included: Degree Certificates, Academic Transcripts, National Police Checks, Personal Identification, Employment Contracts, Professional Body Membership Certificates, and even my secondary school qualifications. All of which took time to meticulously amass and then scan in kind. God forbid I accidentally attach the wrong file in the wrong place, or misspell my surname and date of birth, I thought to myself. It turns out that I shouldn't have worried because my employer had beaten me to it, by putting the wrong date of birth on my VISA nomination application months earlier.

Sometimes, the real troubles in your life are apt to be things that never cross your worried mind. I looked like Edvard Munch's the Scream for days after this mistake came to my attention, post-VISA application, however, I am pleased to tell you that this is not where my story ends. The Australian Government actually granted my VISA two days later, much to me and my employer's surprise. I was elated and jaded in equal measure, because securing the VISA meant that getting to Australia was no longer an endurance event, it was a sprint against the clock.

V

"EVENTS, MY DEAR BOY, EVENTS"

My 482 VISA was medium stream; which meant that I had four years on it. The clock started counting down, on those four precious years, on the month that the VISA had been granted in October 2020. This meant that the longer I was stuck in the UK, the less time I would have in Australia so the faster I could get there the better. There were still two things standing in my way at this point: Firstly, I didn't have a travel exemption. Secondly, I needed to catch a flight to Australia. In 2020, flights to Australia from the UK were sparse and highly volatile with flight cancellations being enacted on a daily basis. Furthermore, I wasn't the only one trying to get out to Oz at this point. Qantas had been running select repatriation flights throughout 2020 to rescue Australian citizens, who had been trapped abroad by the pandemic, and return them home. However, in November there were still estimated to be over thirty-six thousand trapped Australians around the world, waiting to be rescued, hundreds of whom were officially registered as being in a vulnerable state and were rightfully receiving priority.

To make life more awkward, to apply for a travel exemption you needed to provide evidence that you had serious intent to travel to Australia, in the near future. This meant putting your money where your mouth was by buying a one-way ticket to Oz, and then attaching the flight itinerary and e-ticket as evidence in your application. Furthermore, assuming that you did get your hands on a travel exemption, and your flight wasn't cancelled, before boarding a plane to Australia all passengers had to present a negative COVID 19 PCR Swab result, from a test taken and processed at an accredited laboratory, no earlier than seventy-two hours before the time of boarding. This meant that flight cancellations were twice as damaging to the psyche, because one could not exist without the other. If your flight was cancelled, you had to move your PCR swab test appointment, and if your PCR swab test appointment was cancelled, you had to rearrange your flight. No exceptions.

Long story short, I got the travel exemption as quickly as I was granted the VISA. Mercifully, the online application form was only a few pages long this time, and only necessitated thirteen pieces of supporting documentation, most of which I already had. For the intent to travel I ended up gambling on a one-way economy ticket, for a British Airways (BA) flight, that was due to leave for Sydney from London Heathrow on 19/1/21. I am saddened to inform you that I was not on that plane. The dance that ensued, for the next few months, is best presented through the email conversations that I had with Australia while she eagerly awaited my arrival.

2/12/2020

Me: I have booked a new flight for the 1st of February. BA have now cancelled everything to Australia until March, so I have begun the process of acquiring a refund from them. In the meantime, I have booked another flight (with Qatar this time) who had more flight options (all of which were more expensive by £400 minimum) but that was the price of getting an economy flight without a further two month wait, and a sixteen-hour layover. It also means I am released from relying on BA again. Qatar by comparison have been flying planes throughout the entire pandemic, so hopefully this will be a safer bet; although every date seems hypothetical until you are sat on the plane at this stage.

Australia: I hope lock down is treating you well. We are slowly and delicately being released and can now attend group events and such like! Thinking of you!

15/1/2021

Australia: I trust you are well and are in the midst of packing up and organising your affairs. I'm well and just checking in on you. I understand that you may not be able to confirm your status absolutely, however, I am programming our pages for your arrival and entry into our clinic.

Can you assist me to plan by:

1. Providing any form of reassurance/confirmation of your arrival in Australia - Qatar still flying?
2. Date of Exit from quarantine in Sydney - +two weeks
3. Possible starting date
4. Needs

It's an awkward time, and I'm sure, I'll be as much surprised as you when you appear in Australia!

16/1/2021

Me: The third national lockdown, post-Christmas, has been a wake-up call for a lot of people in this country. I feared this would mean more flight cancellations but so far Qatar Airways has stood firm and my flight on the 1st of February still seems to be going ahead. I currently have the following answers and estimations for your questions:

1) I am still acting as if my flight to Sydney will go ahead as booked on the 1st of February at 8:15 am. There is a connection in Qatar, and the plane is estimated to arrive in Sydney on the 2nd of February at 19:05 local time.

2) My understanding is that a person's quarantine begins the morning after they arrive in Australia, so that they have done fourteen full days by the time they are released. For me, I think that will mean that I will begin quarantine on the 3rd of February, and will be released on the 17th of February.

3) My main needs upon arrival will be a place to stay and a means of transport, which I can then use as my postal base to organise everything else (Medicare, Tax file numbers, Australian Driving License, food etc). Currently, I do not have any accommodation booked in Shoalhaven, to tide me over for the first few months upon arrival. So, if you would be able to provide me with some knowledge of anybody in the area who would be willing to take me on as a new tenant, I will then have somewhere to live when the Airport Express drops me off on the 17th of February (hopefully).

25/1/2021

Me: I have just received news that my Qatar flight has been cancelled. I will work on finding a suitable alternative over the next few days and let you know what I can find.

26/1/2021

Me: Okay, my gut feeling based on some wider reading is that airlines serving Australia are being encouraged to discriminate against those with economy tickets. I have attempted to fly out twice now with an economy ticket, with two different airlines, and twice I have got near the finish line only to find that the airline is not able to let me fly, based on one piece of legislation or another. As I understand it, I think that those passengers who are in business seats are being prioritised, to overcome the cap being placed on the number of passengers being allowed to board the final leg of the flight to Australia.

For the third attempt, I have decided to empty the piggy bank and booked a business class journey, which is cheaper than others of its kind because it goes via Zurich and then San Francisco, with some long layovers. This will mean an around the world flight, and I will arrive in Oz with less starting money than I would have ideally liked, but it seems like the best chance I have currently and I suppose it will have to do. Especially with the prospect of continued harsh restrictions on the horizon, which is unlikely to help us along. I now have a Lufthansa flight booked due to leave London on the 12th of February 2021 at 17.55, and land in Sydney on Saturday the 13th of February 2021 at 8:20 am. I am throwing my hat in the ring for the third time. If this doesn't work, I feel that I am out of innovative ideas.

Australia: Oh dear that's terrible news, and well done on securing another flight. I hope you are able to access refunds. Yes, there is a government quota on quarantine, so my understanding is that planes are restricted in their numbers. Your quarantine is self-funded. I'm not sure how this impacts on their numbers, but in my mind, it means as an independent, you possibly are not included in the cap. There is not much info except for media. It's possibly an angle to take. I'll change all our dates and arrangements to suit. Please provide your arrival date in the Shoalhaven. Thanks so much, we are all so looking forward to having you here.

Me: Yes, I was braced for the potential of another punch in the stomach, but a punch in the stomach it was nonetheless. I got a refund quite quickly through PayPal for my original BA flight. I have pursued Qatar Airways for a refund through PayPal as well so hopefully, they will come through again for me. Okay, new working dates would be as follows. If I arrive in Sydney on the Sun 14 Feb 2021, do a two-week quarantine starting from Monday the 15th, this brings us to the 1st of March. If I manage to catch the Airport Express to Shoalhaven on my release day, I will potentially be arriving in the local area on the 1st of March 2021.

27/1/21

Australia: I can't imagine how you are feeling right now. Keep your head up, and your destination in mind. When you are sitting on a beach with white sand and turquoise water and trying to decide whether to swim or just continue basking in the sun, you will know you have arrived. Keep on going! I will plan for the 1/3/21. We can wrap more detail around the clinic schedule once we have a sense of a skills development/supervision plan. Let's work on this while you await your flight. It will be helpful for me to understand where you are at. Let's keep on going, you've made it this far.

SIDE NOTE: To transit through the USA from the UK required something called a VISA Waiver from the U.S. Department of Homeland Security Electronic System for Travel Authorization (ESTA). I did manage to get hold of one of these waivers, at an affordable cost, but as you will see below I never got to use it in the end. It's good until 2023 however, so maybe one day.

28/1/21

Me: I called the US embassy today to get some clarity on UK passengers transiting through the US. In theory, it looked like there was some wiggle room for those who met the candidacy for an ESTA, but it appeared that the current presidential proclamations are unavoidable for the average Joe. The operator at the Embassy was terse but very clear, no UK passengers can transit through the USA period. So, even though flights to the US from the UK can still be booked (confusingly), and authorizations can be granted (also confusingly), you won't be allowed through customs when you get there. Therefore, I have had to cancel the Lufthansa flight I had booked for 12.2.2021.

All the reading and research I have been doing have now led me to the following conclusions. I can't transit through the US, and the presidential proclamations won't be reviewed until March. The traditional transport hubs like Abu Dhabi, Qatar, and Singapore serve more direct flights which are few and far between. There are business class flights in late February; but because they are more direct without significant layovers, they are too expensive for me to book on short notice. Economy tickets are cheaper, but because of the passenger capacity regulations being imposed by the Australian government on airlines, which themselves are not going to be reviewed again until sometime in February I believe, it means that economy passengers are likely to be capped in favour of the business class and 1st class passengers; who spent much more on their ticket and are therefore more costly to the airline to cancel. Furthermore, the capacity cap is often not implemented until two-five days before the flight is due to take off, similar to what I experienced with Qatar, so you start to make plans only to have the rug pulled out from under you.

Qantas is offering repatriation flights from London to Darwin non-stop. Even though I qualify for these flights now, because I have a travel exemption, politically I think the Oz government will be prioritising Australian citizens (quite rightly), who have been trapped abroad since the pandemic hit. Every time I have tried to book on to one of these repatriation flights recently, the system tells me there are no more spaces available. The Oz government does not appear to want to fund more of these repatriation flights, arguing that they are already in debt and the repatriation flights are expensive; so should only be used for emergency or compassionate cases. Those Australians who have made it this far, trapped abroad, must be in a position to wait longer for the pandemic to ease. That could be another year plus, even with the vaccine on the horizon.

In conclusion, I am not sure what to say other than I will keep looking for suitable flights and will try to snag a more direct business class flight if I can, to improve my chances of avoiding the passenger capacity caps. Looking ahead, this may well end up being in March or maybe even April. They all seem to be a roll of the dice, whichever airline I plump for, but maybe if our lockdown in the UK ends and the Oz government ease their capacity caps in February, I will have more luck next time.

I'm sorry that I didn't have better news; every turn I make I seem to hit a brick wall presently.

Australia: Oh dear! This is an interesting situation, I was hoping it wasn't as dire as it is. I must say it's extraordinary that you cannot come via the USA. And yes no doubt during Trumps time probably you could, although the airport might not have been staffed! Interesting times Tom.

So, your options are; an Australian repatriation flight, purchase a direct flight business class ticket, or wait for an undetermined period of time.

My recommendation to you is;

1. Apply for a repatriation flight

2. What are the costs of a direct business class flight in FEB? And then with a longer lead time, march/April?

3. The cap into Australia is all about quarantine budget. If you are independently funding your quarantine, does the cap still apply? How can we get around that?

4. Wait for an election to be called – predicted to be announced soonish… we have had no COVID cases nationally for nearly a fortnight.

It sounds like the limit is the Australian budget. There are flights but limited quarantine budget. If access was increased then repatriation flights could be reduced. To be honest, repatriation flights may only exist for PR; to quench the disgruntlement of the Australian public… And ease the way into an election. I'll look forward to hearing from you.

Me: I will keep looking out for spaces on the repatriation flights. Currently they are only flying up to the 1st of February and these flights appear to be fully booked. If the Oz government do end up funding some more of these, I will keep an eye out and try to snag a seat. I will use Etihad as our example, who now appear to be the only airline consistently flying at the moment. For mid-February (16th of Feb onward) we are looking at £8435.74 (AUS $ 15,143.80). This price is the same until the 10th of March where the price is £4,235.74 (AUS $7603.98), but only for that day. It returns to £8435.74 again for the rest of March and April. The prices consistently become £4,235.74 once you get to May and beyond. The cap would appear to apply to anybody who is trying to enter Australia, and it is up to the government which passengers they choose to let in. For my ticket with Qatar, the government would have known what I am coming in for and that I am not a citizen, so I would have to fund my own quarantine, but I didn't make the cut anyway. The airlines are obligated to give the Oz government their passenger's details before they fly, so the fact that I was paying for my own quarantine would not appear to have been enough for me to make the cut. This would infer there are other reasons at play. Here is what Qatar had to say: *"The passenger list is continually assessed and based on a range of criteria, including compassionate and medical requests, connecting flights, booking class, party size etc."* I am hoping to get my Qatar refund by the 9th of February, and my Lufthansa refund within the next seven days if they perform as advertised.

29/1/2021

Australia: Wow! Yes that is expensive. In a do what you can to get over here in a difficult set of circumstances, and given you have tried all possible avenues. Would it help if we went fifty per cent with you? I totally understand not wanting to pay out $15k on a one-way flight. I couldn't budget for that either. But if we split the cost, and I matched whatever you are willing to pay (Certainly I'd encourage you toward the 10th of March). The March the 10th flight looks great! How would that sit with you?

Me: I would appreciate any help that you are in a position to provide, the complexities of this situation are outmanoeuvring me at every turn. fifty/fifty on the cheapest business plane ticket would be very welcome. Assuming that the deal for March the 10th is still there by the time I get my refund back, from Qatar and Lufthansa, with your assistance I will operate under the assumption that I can book it ASAP. Unfortunately, the cost of the Lufthansa ticket cleared out my instant access savings. So, until I get that back, going fifty per cent on a new ticket will put me in overdraft. I will keep pestering Lufthansa and will start up a PayPal dispute if they drag their feet.

Australia: Happy to help you get on that early flight, I've managed to book that ticket for the 21.3.21. Good luck! We will sort out the payment perhaps when you are in Australia, and you can reimburse me in Australian Dollars.

Me: Thank you for helping me out with this. I have attached all of the Etihad booking information that I have received.

12/3/2021

Me: I contacted Etihad about my upcoming flight, and I was advised that the best thing to do would be to put any additional information, about my circumstances, on the Australian government travel declaration form that I have to submit before

I fly. According to the Oz government website, the declaration has to be submitted between three-seven days before the flight. What I will do is on the 14th of March, I will submit the declaration including the information about my quarantine being privately funded, and about the fact that I will have received part 2 of the Pfizer-BioNTech COVID 19 vaccine by the time I leave the UK. That way the Oz government will have had the most time to see it, hopefully before they begin finalizing their passenger capacity regulations on upcoming flights.

Australia: That's all good. Great you have had both parts of the vaccine. I'll wait for your news.

17/3/2021

Me: So far so good and no bad news from Etihad. I have had my Part 2 Pfizer jab now, so that went as planned. I will get my pre-flight COVID PCR swab tomorrow. It's a slightly moot thing really because I've heard that some airlines will swab you at the airport, before you board the plane. So, in theory even with your negative test certificate, if you test positive right before boarding they won't let you fly anyway.

22/3/2021

Australia: Did you get a seat on the flight?

VI

DOES THIS LOOK INFECTED?

I did catch a plane that day, which was an endeavour in itself because God had not stopped laughing yet. I awoke on the day of departure to find that I had developed a stye in one of my right eyelash roots. This could not have come at a worse time because one look that I didn't want to mimic, at Heathrow Airport during a COVID 19 pandemic, was the look of an infected person. There is something about diseases of the eye that are incredibly noticeable. It's right where people are encouraged to look when they speak to you, and they cause a marked facial asymmetry highlighted by redness and swelling. I couldn't have looked more infectious if I'd tried, but it was too late to turn back now. I took combined nurofen and paracetamol to numb the pain, squeezed as much pus out of the stye as I could reach, with TCP sterilised fingers, washed away the discharge with warm water from an eyewash cup, prayed that my mask would help to hide the rest and we were off. We being my Dad and I.

Dad always tends to be my last goodbye, and in keeping with tradition he had volunteered to take me to the airport, which by this point had been over two years in the making. After waving him off at the drop zone feeling: heavy hearted, nervous and intrepid all at once, I made my way into the departures terminal. I was quite scared of immediate ejection to start with, in the unnerving masked emptiness of what used to be a bustling

38

London check-in terminal, but once I had a human being in front of me at the check-in desk I began to calm down. The attendant at my check-in desk asked me for my: passport, negative COVID 19 PCR swab test result, and my VISA. I was also asked to drop my mask so that she could compare my face to the picture on my passport, which I did reticently fearing what was to come. She did not mention the stye even if she noticed it. I loved her for that.

The attendant then asked me for my travel declaration, which wasn't a problem I thought because I had printed a hard copy of the digital declaration, which I had submitted on the Australian Government's website, days earlier. She then drained all the colour from my face when she had finished examining this hard copy and said: *"Not this one, Sir, where is your individual declaration for leaving the UK?"* I was completely unprepared for this eventuality, because I had no idea which document she was talking about. My whole world fell apart for a second right there at the check-in desk, until she smiled and said: *"not to worry, you can do one here by hand it's quite simple"*. I was advised to carry this UK declaration with me at all times, as I navigated my way through the airport, so I stashed it away like a precious jewel. The lady then disappeared to make a phone call to a government official, in Australia, to check whether my name was on their travel exemption database. This probably only took a few minutes but it felt like several hours, and I don't know what would have happened if my name had not been on the list when the call came through, but it was, so I happily consigned that eventuality to the multi-verse. I checked my luggage, was told to enjoy my flight, and headed around the corner to security.

The only issue I had at security was with the dental picks, which I had forgotten to remove from the bottom pocket of my wash bag. When the cockney sounding security officer asked me whether there was anything else sharp in there, he had laughed raucously when I answered: *'tweezers'*, quite earnestly. I was allowed to keep my dental picks so I made my way to the unchartered waters of the Etihad business class lounge, where I discovered that everything is complimentary, and the buffet is all you can eat. Full English breakfast, Twinning's tea, orange juice, soft drinks, croissants, comfortable chairs, numerous and accessible wall sockets, Wi-Fi, and fruit cocktails. Lovely. I kept asking for things with the half expectation that it could all be up for debate, but the staff simply obliged me and waited for my next command. As I looked around, I saw a lounge filled with a mix of (mostly white) single travellers, couples and families. I also overheard glimpses of official looking men debating important topics such as: the population of Japan, Newcastle United, China, and the challenges of new girlfriends. There are worse ways to wait for your flight. I was even impressed when I left the lounge through the secret sliding door, which I realised upon exit had been camouflaged to blend in with the terminal wall, when viewed from the outside. I felt like Bruce Wayne.

I had never turned left on an aeroplane before, and I will admit to you without hesitation that it lives up to the hype. In the happy land of business class nothing seemed to be too much trouble: this was fully demonstrated to me when I ordered off-menu quite by accident. Every mealtime had a unique set of options to choose from, and the menu never repeated itself. Steak for instance, was an option that would appear on the menu only once during the flight. However, after admitting quite innocently to the flight attendant, after enjoying my steak: *"that was so tasty I would quite happily have that again"* she took this as a literal request and said: *"I'll check"*. Before I knew what had happened, she had swept away to check whether any spare steaks were available for me to have as my next meal. Two flight attendants returned minutes later, beaming beneath their masks, to tell me: *"the answer is yes"*, and they took care to ensure that I was served steak again for my next meal. Cop for that! From that point forth, I learned to pick my moments before examining the various menus available to me, out of pure curiosity, because if one of the flight attendants caught me at it I could expect that to be taken as a request for service.

The first leg of the flight, and the subsequent connection that ended it, was smooth apart from a random bag search in Abu Dhabi at Gate 35 Terminal 3. Two men in military uniform, and one man in a white thobe, evacuated us from the waiting area and asked us to line up outside single file. We were then instructed to re-enter the waiting area one at a time and present our carry-on luggage to two serious looking women, in police uniform, paying close attention to present all of our electrical items and chargers. Fortunately, it was all fine and I was given the all clear to board. Arriving in Sydney was an intimidating experience, even though the staff who are waiting for you do try to minimise the fright. I was first debriefed by a nurse who gave me the 411 on what would happen to me during my time in the quarantine hotel. She then gave me an orange customs declaration form, before directing me to walk along an expansive lane of rope barriers which snaked their way through a ghost town of empty terminals, until I reached the immigration check-in desk.

At the immigration desk lived a poker-faced woman, who took my passport to check whether my real face matched my

41

passport picture, for an unnervingly long time. I was having a good face day it would seem, because she waved me onward to the luggage carousel. I was pleased to see that my favourite Guatemalan palm leaf hat had made the journey along with me, damage free. After I gathered my personal effects, it was on to customs.

Regarding Australian Customs, I have a top tip. Based on my experience of landing in Perth, back in 2019, Australian Customs Officials seem to treat you less suspiciously if you declare something. I would advise any of you to declare something, even if you don't think you have anything to declare. My go to item in this situation is soap, and I take care to declare it whenever I arrive in Oz, complete with the verbal admission that it is made from animal fats and might therefore be significant. Which it is technically. However, based on the fact that the customs official in Perth simply chuckled at me when I declared it to him quite in earnest, before he waved me straight on through, I now declare a bar of soap every time without fail. In Perth, those who declared nothing at all seemed to be having their bags opened and searched by gloved officials, and Sydney proved to be no different.

A man approached me, whilst I was queueing, to inspect my orange form and ask me whether I had anything to declare. I declared my bar of soap, and the potentially significant animal fats that it was composed of, and he said: *"ah no worries on that one mate"* with a dismissive shake of the head, before attaching a green label to my luggage. The customs screening area reminded me of a biochemical luggage morgue. Suitcases were all being clinically laid out on stainless steel tables, to be dissected by men and women in: masks, gloves, and hair nets. But not mine. One custom official took one look at the green label on my luggage and pointed me towards a large masked man in a bulletproof vest, holding a machine gun. I approached him, now worrying that the green label attached to my suitcase must have said: *'shoot this man on sight'*, but he simply instructed me to turn left; where I was surprised to see sliding glass doors marked with an exit sign. I was out.

The heavens were open in Sydney that night, and I was greeted by another slightly wet looking military checkpoint as I exited the terminal. This checkpoint had a slightly ad-hoc theme because it consisted of two uniformed army women, sporting umbrellas, stationed at what was unmistakably a fold out camping table. I was issued with a bag of masks along with some more paperwork to complete on the coach. I was privileged to be the first man on to the coach, which gave me a unique vantage point to count just how many other people had made it to Sydney that evening, as they boarded one at a time. There were only eighteen, which I think is quite extraordinary because I came in on a jumbo jet after all. Furthermore, not all eighteen made it on to the coach. I distinctly remember one couple with two small children being held back at the checkpoint, as we all drove away into the night.

I never did find out what happened to them. The coach drove through the darkness to an unfamiliar hotel in an unknown location, where a police sergeant boarded to give us a talk on the legal consequences of leaving our room, during the quarantine period. We were promised heavy fines if we did so, to the tune of thousands of dollars. After he was finished, a hotel representative boarded to explain what the room service could provide, and what the hotel rules were. He was heckled mid-way through his descriptions, by an agitated man, who wished to express his displeasure at the prospect of not having a window from which to smoke cigarettes, during his quarantine.

After the coach debrief, we were taken four at a time into the hotel lobby. Four police officers were waiting for us in the lobby, one for each of us. I was asked for the paperwork that I had filled out on the coach; which highlighted the work and residential addresses which I proposed to travel to after completing my quarantine. I also presented my passport. I was asked to place each document into a wicker basket and then slide them through a letterbox sized gap, in the plastic shield, which separated me from the officer perched at the other end of the table. He was: young, polite, and slightly timid which was welcome. The Scottish passenger next to me, who was a Farrier from Glasgow by trade, was unfortunately making himself quite unintelligible to a much fiercer looking seasoned female officer; who subsequently insisted on inspecting his boarding pass, which is not something that I had to present. After I cleared the police checkpoint, another military man appeared with the objective of escorting me to my cell in room 855.

"Do me a favour mate, kick that doorstop out from under there, would you, once you're in". I did as I was told and he retreated behind the closing door, which clicked shut undeniably. Silence ensued, and my quarantine began.

VII

EVICTION IS YOUR REWARD

Sydney is not the capital of Australia, but it's certainly one of the beating hearts. Not that I saw any of it during my quarantine. I eventually figured out that I was serving my time at a Novotel on Darling Harbour, which is in close proximity to all the classics like: The Opera House, Sydney Harbour Bridge, King Street Wharf etc. but my room was not high enough to catch a glimpse above the vast expanse of residential buildings, which are plentiful. My window permitted a view that enabled me to become intimately familiar with my neighbours daily: exercise, breakfast, and laundry routines, all performed from the stage of their enviable balconies overhanging Murray Street. As a self-confessed introvert, two weeks in solitary confinement was not the end of the world for me, but I know others who were quarantined that found it memorably distressing. Being imprisoned in a guarded hotel room, without direct human contact, and a finite choice of dietary options doesn't suit everyone. All I can say to that is that hardship, like many human experiences, is relative. I can also say that the secret to surviving quarantine is to form a daily routine as quickly as possible, regardless of how pedestrian your activities are. There is nothing quite like a daily routine to nurture a perception of time passing at an accelerated rate, and it provides a thread of normality through otherwise unfamiliar settings.

Ten minutes after the military man closed the door behind me, on Day 0, there was a curt knock at the door to signify that food had arrived. I masked up and opened the door to find a brown paper bag, on the floor, with my room number on it. Its contents included a hot meal and some dessert all packaged neatly in plastic tubs. On Day two, I had the first of my in-house PCR swab tests; this was applied to both nostrils, and the back of my throat, by plastic encased medical staff sporting a stainless-steel trolley. Not completely unlike a cavity search for new prisoners, you must first sound off your name and date of birth, before answering some questions about whether you are suffering from new flu-like symptoms. You must then assume the position: mask down, chin up, back against the door. This enables maximum penetration, for the person brandishing the long swab, when they plumb the depths of your respiratory passages. If it didn't bring a tear to your eye, it wasn't deep enough! I was told that no news was good news, and if I heard from the medical team again that day it meant that I was sick and should await further instructions.

On the 1st of April, around the midpoint of my quarantine, I received a surprise call from room service enquiring whether it was my birthday. It turned out that a box of doughnuts had just turned up and that the Uber Eats driver was adamant that it was for a man called Alex, living in room 855. Unfortunately, I had to confess that my name was Tom and my birthday was not until April 29th, but being cheeky I would still be happy to eat the doughnuts if they were not claimed. I never received those doughnuts, so I assumed they must have been claimed. Two days later I received a text from Alex, my brother, asking whether I had enjoyed my tasty Easter surprise, which he had organised for me as a quarantine treat. So it goes. Room service confirmed that they had all been thrown out by then, much to my chagrin.

The other piece of news that I received from the hotel,

46

around the midpoint of my quarantine, was more perturbing because it turned out that traces of a COVID 19 strain had been found on the plane that I had arrived on. This now meant that in addition to my orthodox Day two and Day ten swabs, I would also need to pass a Day twelve swab before I could be released. The Day ten swab managed to interrupt an induction ZOOM call with my boss in Shoalhaven, fortunately the knock at the door came near the end of the chat so it could have been worse. On Day thirteen, a Doctor came to the door to place a plastic band around my wrist, and informed me that it was waterproof so I could shower with it on. He also issued me with some paperwork to prove that I had met the quarantine requirements set down by the NSW government.

I was also visited that day by a man from the military, with a lazy eye and a cap, who informed me that I could leave the premises on Day fourteen either in the morning or in the evening, and that if I needed help with my bags then I should call room service. We agreed on 5pm, which was half an hour before my pre-booked Shoalhaven minibus was due to arrive. Later that same evening, a red eviction notice was thrust under my door which jumpstarted my heart, until I realised that it was in jest: *"By order of Novotel Sydney on Darling Harbour, we hereby advise that you are evicted from the hotel, the reason for this eviction notice is: you have successfully completed your 14-day quarantine"*. The gut-wrenching startle reflex evoked by the red capital letters, headlining this A4 piece of paper, proved to me that I was obviously still irrationally panicked about being shipped back to the UK. Despite successfully waking up in Sydney every day for the past two weeks, confirming that it wasn't all a dream.

I was the last person on my floor to leave the hotel on Day

fourteen. My last meal was a good one, which came in the form of a deluxe Aussie burger complete with: lettuce, tomato, beetroot, bacon, eggs, and chunky chips. No alarms went off when I crossed the threshold to the corridor, and I saw no signs of additional cameras. As I approached the elevator however, I did come across an overweight security guard with an equally large radio. *"What's your number?"* he asked *"855"* I answered. He raised the radio to his mouth *"we have 855 coming down"*, *"righto"* crackled the response from downstairs. I stepped decorously into the elevator where nothing happened for an embarrassingly long time. It took me a while to realise that the reason for this was because I had not pressed any of the buttons. During quarantine I had apparently forgotten how elevators worked. When the doors eventually opened on the ground floor, I was pointed to another police checkpoint composed of: three officers and three laptops. A rapid game of eeny, meeny, miny, mo took me to the third officer from the left, where I was asked to present my passport and my post-quarantine paperwork. After much: typing, clicking, and searching glances, my documents were returned and I was shown the glass side door leading to the outside world. My first quarantine was over, and I was free.

VIII

THE ONLY ONE LIKE ME

Stepping out on to the balmy streets of Sydney, catching the light of the sunset, was surreal. I had come from the old world, and was therefore accustomed to wearing masks almost everywhere I went in public. Now suddenly, I could see the bottom half of every persons face as they walked by, which is something that I had not witnessed for over twelve months. It's pathetic to admit but I was slightly shocked, like a man in the 1890s who had just witnessed a woman showing her ankles. Sydney felt like I had taken a time machine back to a period before anybody had even heard of COVID 19. I didn't quite know how to be, I felt like a bilingual person who suddenly had to start speaking French again, after a year of only speaking Spanish. The minibus that I had booked to take me south to Sanctuary Point arrived bang on time, and the driver jumped out to meet me. *"How ya goin, I'm Jeff"* he said. *"I'm Tom"* I replied, *"hey Tommy"*. Jeff nicknamed instinctively before helping me load up my bags. Nicknaming, just like cricket, is very much an Australian pastime.

Seeing as we weren't strangers anymore, I hopped on board. Jeff informed me that his old lady had managed to escape the floods, which had swamped NSW over the past two weeks, and that the plagues of mice were not as bad as the media had made out. I took him at his word, because I had no alternative. He also told me that we had two other people to pick up, at Sydney

Airport, before we began the two-and-a-half-hour journey south. There was a Liverpudlian; who was on her way to the naval station HMAS Albatross, and a returning Australian; his white beard billowed around his COVID mask like Gandalf from Lord of the Rings. If only wizards wore shorts. I was the last to be dropped off at my destination, which was after dark by the time we arrived. The lady, who had agreed to take me in during my first few weeks in Australia, was there to greet me.

I still remember how deafeningly loud the cicadas rang out through the air that night, as I was invited into the bungalow. I had only spoken to my new landlord via email up until that point, and we had only been introduced half way through my quarantine. She was a friend of my new boss, whom she had met through an art connection. Victoria was her name and she was like a living Matryoshka Doll, the more we spoke the more versions of herself she revealed. She was the daughter of a diplomat, and she owed her Aussie citizenship to her Dad but had actually spent most of her childhood years moving from country to country, due to her father's diplomatic responsibilities, along with her mother and brother. She eventually left home at fifteen and travelled to Canberra; she worked as a waitress and lived alongside a woman who had the annoying habit of stealing dresses. Eventually, she joined the circus as a backing singer, where she travelled in convoy up and down the entire east coast, with her new boyfriend 'Ape-o'; so called because he entertained audiences by dressing up in a gorilla costume and nobody knew his real name.

The circus disbanded after a chaotic shambles; attributable to the majority of the performers electing to drop acid before going out on stage one night. Many of the audience members left in shock, and Victoria never saw Ape-o again. After her time in the circus, she bummed around Sydney for a while before deciding to go back to school to get her diploma, after being saved by her brother during a near death experience; the exact details of which remain a mystery. As luck would have it her father had recently been posted to Brussels, where his diplomatic position in the ranks granted his extended family the chance of a university education at art school. Despite not speaking French fluently at the time, Victoria moved to Brussels and signed up. Unfortunately, she never got the chance to finish her qualification because her father was posted to another country, one year later, and the university funding subsequently dried up.

Not to be discouraged, Victoria started to work as an artist crafting invitations and designing menus for local businesses. As fate would have it this is how she met her future life partner; she was working as a photographer and he was working as an artist. A married man at the time, he had been kicked out by his current wife for kissing another woman. Victoria informed me that he was not French, but he had a French mind-set: *"I don't know what the problem is"* he had apparently said at the time. They worked together on a joint project for twelve months. During their courtship, she was often believed to be his daughter, as he was twenty years her senior. One lady, who interestingly enough claimed that she was the love child of the Duke of Edinburgh, once said to Victoria: *'I am very interested in your Daddy'*. This same lady once invited Victoria's partner over for a so-called 'meeting', and during proceedings asked him to fetch her a glass of water from the kitchen. When he returned she was naked on the sofa. He double took, and all lust that may have been in his body drained in that very moment. Victoria and her partner eventually went on to buy an enormous farm house together, in the French countryside, where they lived happily for a long time. When he died Victoria decided to sell up and return to Australia, in August 2020, after thirty years of living abroad.

Back in the present Victoria explained to me, over a glass of

Prosecco, that the reason she decided to take me in was because she knew what I was in for. Having only moved back to Australia herself months earlier, to start her life again, she took pity on me as a fellow *"blow in"* and knew that I would need the kindness of strangers. Just as she had needed the kindness of her friends in Sydney; who put her up while she was organising the build of her new house. She was absolutely right. I drank more wine during my time living with Victoria then I had in my entire life. She snored like a chainsaw and only charged me $260 a week all-inclusive. She was an empathetic witness to my existence while I learned to walk in those first few months, and explained to me that it would take six before I stopped asking myself *"what the hell have I done?"* But she reassured me that when I call a friend or family member back home, the haze would clear from my mind, and in time would subside forever.

"Australians only really care about Australia", she warned me *"and have little comprehension of international accomplishments"*. *"They do not give a shit about how hard it is for blow-ins to get by when they first arrive. You should know everything we know already, and so what if they do it differently elsewhere"*. Victoria knew two Australians, who once took a trip around Europe, whose subsequent take on it when they returned home was the following: *"Europe was shit; there were too many churches and not enough toppings on the pizzas"*. *"You must have air-con and heating'* Victoria professed *"and remember that it's the estate agents job to resist questions, and any requests to adjust what is advertised on the prelease"*.

In addition to drinking much wine from her extensive collection, and making me delicious home cooked meals from scratch using her father's recipe book. Victoria's love of the kitchen was only overshadowed by the love she had for her golden retrievers, and for the card game Bridge which she could play in many styles including: French, Australian and American.

She didn't thank me when I managed to scratch one of her non-stick frying pans, by somehow managing to break all of the rules for using nonstick cookware in one session. Do not use high heat, I used high heat. No metal implements, I used metal implements. No sharp objects to turn the meat over, I did that too because I couldn't find the nylon tongs. I purchased some new pans to say sorry, and we reconciled over some brie. She even let me keep the scratched frying pan to serve as a house warming gift, to use in my new domicile.

I got very lucky finding a rental townhouse just up the road from where Victoria lived, right before she was due to visit friends in Melbourne for two weeks. Quite understandably, she did not want a still relative stranger living in her pristinely furnished Bungalow whilst she was away. Furthermore, Victoria admitted to me some time later that by this point in time, she had begun to feel claustrophobic having not been used to living in such close quarters, with a stranger, for many years. Also, quite coincidentally, my presence in her life eventually came to serve as a reminder of the pain that she was experiencing, from the realisation that a friendship that she had forged months earlier, founded on what she thought was an appreciation of her as a person, had actually been founded on an appreciation of the lucrative opportunities that she could provide as a person. All things considered, it was time for me to go.

The property that I was successful in applying for allegedly had forty other applicants, and I was shocked to find that what I was getting was an empty shell. No washing machine, no heater, no air conditioning, and no furniture. It was the biggest property I had ever lived in, but it was completely empty. In the UK, every rental property that I had resided in had been furnished upon arrival. That's when I understood why Australians love K-mart so much, it took a lot of weekend shopping trips there to get what I needed. The other thing that the estate agent had to explain to me, after I had baffled her by asking whether she could tell me which utility provider I should contact to arrange a meter reading, is that gas meters are not a thing out in the sticks. The people of Sanctuary Point rely on truck deliveries of 45 kg Liquefied Petroleum Gas (LPG) bottles, which are attached to taps on the outside of their properties. My townhouse also had a Rheem 170 litre LPG outdoor water heater, attached to the decking. Other than the fact that high winds would often blow out the pilot light, it also had the disadvantage of a refractory period. After what was undeniably a very powerful ten-minute shower the water would suddenly go ice cold, and you would then have to give the tank about an hour to refill and for the water to re-heat, before using it again.

I still vividly remember calling up the company Red Energy; who take care to advertise themselves as one hundred per cent Australian, because I had inappropriately booked a direct line gas metre check on my property. I was very tickled at the irony of an unmistakably Indian man answering the phone that day. I'd like to think that Alanis Morrisette would have appreciated the naff parody to her lyrics, for the hit song, Ironic, that popped into my head soon afterward: *'it's like an Indian man, who's on the phone. At a hundred per cent, Australian company. And who would have thought… it figures…* Teething problems with the property when I moved in meant that there was only electricity provided to one half of the house, which delayed certain aspects of my move somewhat, but nevertheless I was in. Furthermore, once I had an airbed and figured out that the ungodly noises, that pierced the silence of the night, were not poltergeists but mating Brushtail Possums. I started to settle into my new routine and make myself at home.

IX

MEET THE NEW BOSS

Dr Martens. They were the shoes that I was wearing for my first day on the job in Australia. They were oxblood, with two large cracks in the right Good Year welt, and black kinesiology tap wrapped around the inside of the heel; patching where the leather had eroded away. They had travelled a long way from the UK those shoes, and wearing them gave me a sense of continuity in what was otherwise a whole new world. Victoria was kind enough to drop me off on my first day, because I soon discovered that destinations in Australia look deceptively close together on google maps. I soon abandoned my naïve notion of walking to work when I discovered that it would take me ninety minutes.

My new boss was not there to greet me on my first day, but luckily the woman with whom I would form arguably the most pivotal of friendships with, during my time in Sanctuary Point, was. Her name was Tracy. Tracy had the keys to my chariot. The company car that I inherited was a Robin Egg Blue Daihatsu Sirion, 5 speed manual, from 2003. It was meant to be used by my new work colleagues to do weekly postal runs with for the clinic. I later found out that most of them avoided it like the plague because it was a manual; they preferred driving their own automatics. The Daihatsu came complete with what classic car enthusiasts tend to describe as character traits, which included the following:

- A gearbox as sticky as treacle, which once jumped out of

gear when I was driving up a hill, just to check if my adrenaline glands were still operational.

• The plastic panel underneath the ignition switch was taped in place.

• The carpet in the foot well on the driver's side was worn down to the metal, and the loose replacement covering rug would roll up underneath the pedals whilst driving.

• The serpentine belt needed replacing which caused the car to squeal like a pig during acceleration, and after braking. It once squealed so loudly that it caused a small child to pull on her mother's coat pockets in alarm, as I drove past them both in a local Woolworth's car park.

• The electric window control switch on the driver's side was intermittent, so if you were not careful it would disconnect after rolling the window down, leaving the inside of the car exposed to: the weather, insects, and thieves. I ended up disconnecting the control switch in the end, to save the risk.

• Unnervingly rough engine idling when sat in traffic.

• It was also gutless, and had no power for motorway driving.

And the cherry on the cake, it had a bright yellow and orange sticker on the windscreen which said the word 'Shitbox' on it. Despite all of its character flaws, it was still better than walking so I welcomed it with open arms.

On my second day at work, I was met with a handshake and a mountain of new starter paperwork courtesy of my new, soon to be estranged, boss. On Day 4, it soon crystallised that I was expected to drive straight into clinic duties, unsupervised, which can only be described as a baptism of fire. Suffice to say, even though the healthcare needs of human beings around the world are universal, the rules and regulations of healthcare systems around the world are significantly different. It took several

56

months to get my head around the Australian healthcare system, and it was an unforgettably stressful time. I made it through on: clinical instinct, faith that I would get better and the process would get easier if I just kept showing up, and by doing what my all-knowing clerical team told me to do. Karen if you're reading this, I would have been lost without your quiet empathy and insight. It took two months before I had become efficient enough, to afford a lunch break with sufficient time, to make and drink my first cup of tea on the 7th of June 2021. A glorious moment.

I had to be very honest with myself during this period of time. I had essentially spent the previous two years convincing the Australian Government that I was the best of the best. Only to arrive and realise that I really knew nothing. It's very deceptive. I was seeing what I thought were familiar things, but I was now in a commercialised healthcare environment. Even though the jungle looked the same, the climate was completely different. James Dunlop once said to me that it's hard to teach men how to skydive, because it's in their nature to fight against the wind. They instinctively press their hands against the thrust of the fan, and end up flying off at different angles. It took me three weeks to properly accept that I was back at school and had to once again give myself to the currents in order to advance. Australia had gained my potential, not my immediate prowess, because what good is Earth's greatest navigator when you're lost on Mars.

Now that I was working, and renting, I needed to be paid an Australian salary. To be paid an Australian salary I required an Australian bank account. As a migrant in rural NSW, this meant that I had to drive one hour and thirty minutes to my nearest migrant friendly branch in Wollongong. When I got there, I needed to present my passport, my occupational details, and my UK national insurance number to one of their customer service specialists. Most leading banks in rural Australia are open

Monday to Friday 9:30am till 4pm, sometimes till 5pm if you're lucky. CommBank had allowed me to begin the registration process for an Australian bank account online, whilst I was still in the UK, and they were open on a Saturday morning between ten a.m. to two p.m. On one such Saturday morning, I was able to secure an audience with Kylie (not that one), who was indeed one of CommBank's customer service specialists. Four hours seemed like ample time to achieve my goal, but there was a problem.

CommBank required an Australian phone number to complete the migrant bank account registration process, using SMS text message confirmation. For my first few weeks in Australia I had been making use of Vodafone global roaming, tied to my UK phone number, which could not be accepted. Australian banking networks do not appreciate international dialling codes it would appear, which meant once again that the race was on. After reassurances from Kylie that she would do her best Connie Francis impression, by waiting for me, I charged though Wollongong Central frantically searching for a Vodafone shop; so that I could start up a new contract before they closed early. I had to get a new contract, activate the new Australian number, and get back to CommBank before they closed. There was a queue in the Vodafone shop, which in the heat of the moment seemed to last an eternity, but I eventually got the new contract, activated my new Australian phone number, and charged back to Kylie who finished the registration process with just under thirty minutes to spare. Nothing is ever easy it would seem, although having an Australian bank account opened up everything else including: Superannuation, Medicare, and a Tax File Number. They were all much easier online application affairs by comparison.

X

SERENDIPITY

You know it's funny what a young man recollects. I don't remember being born, I don't recall what I got for my first Christmas, and I don't know where I went on my first outdoor picnic, but I do remember all of the different people that I met during my time as an Audiologist in Shoalhaven. I don't know much about anything but I think I met some of Australia's best during those four months. There was Peter, the ex-doorman that survived a heart attack on the streets of London. He brought my attention to one of the most inappropriate road signs currently erected on the Wool Road, linking Sanctuary Point to Vincentia, warning locals to watch out for wombats. Peter had lived in Sanctuary Point for several decades and had never seen a Wombat. He and every other driver in Sanctuary Point knows that it's not the wombats you have to watch out for, it's the kangaroos and the Q fever they carry that'll get ya.

There was Tony, now retired and acting as a full-time carer to his wife. He used to be a manager in charge of quality control for a multi-national corporation. A self-confessed curmudgeon: *"I'm not the easiest bugger to get along with",* he once said to me, which was correct. His travels had taken him across the South China Sea to the Hyundai factory in South Korea, and he still endeavoured to enact his grand thirty five-year plans of going walkabout 200km south of Alice Springs, and 40km north of the South Australian border, to discover the Lambert Centre of

Australia. Also known as the geographical dead centre of the Australian continent. *"Go bush"* he told me *"it's beautiful. It's flat, baron trees and harsh but it's beautiful in its own way. Everybody wants to do the coast when they come to Australia, but you can do that in any country. You might as well be in Brighton or some other place right, go bush. My relatives come over here and they say, no we want to see Cairns and Townsville or some other place and I think sod em. Go bush. You'll need a 4 x 4 mind".*

My travels also took me south, to the town of Ulladulla, to see Craig the menswear shop owner. Craig also catered to ladies on the side, if said ladies desired clothing that was narrow in the hip and broad in the shoulder of course. Craig was of the old school of tailoring, he could unashamedly size you up with a radar stare, and drop your ego around your ankles with a single conclusion: *"you look like a man who likes his clothes to be loose fitting"* and *"you are not little are you, you're solid".* Not encumbered by a need for measuring tapes, Craig fingered through the shirts on the rack before exclaiming: *"I just need to see it on you and then I will know if it fits right away. This is the style that you want, bomb proof elasticated waist. Will last a lifetime".* You might think that such a bold approach would evoke resistance from those customers who thought of their body shapes differently, in their own heads, but Craig had a power move. He could hold a shirt aloft with one hand and systematically undo all the buttons on said shirt from top to bottom, with the other hand, all the while maintaining eye contact with you and without breaking his conversational stride. For uncultured men like me who sometimes fumble when doing their shirt buttons up with two hands, I was under no illusions who the daddy was in Craig's shop.

I was ushered away to a fitting cubicle by Craig's assistant, and I was not half way done undressing myself before the curtain flew open behind me, exposing my choice of underwear to the shop in the process: *"How's my Englishman, whoa that ones for free, we like the customers to get their value for money"*. I eventually left the cubicle a little time after my premature reveal, so that I could present myself to Craig for judgement: *"XL shirt, yeah expansive waist and short leg, you are pretty easy to dress."* He was right, I could not deny that I was comfortable and mobile within the newly fitted clothing he had chosen for me. His parting words as I left the shop were: *"You will get a fair amount of flack; all the pommes do"*.

I purchased my first three-piece suite from Tash, a single mother from Canberra, who now resided in a gated community guarded by an enormous black gate, controlled by a panel which I learned upon arrival was stuck on Spanish. All those who approached had to navigate the user interface which only gave Spanish prompts, before typing in the access code to gain entry. Tash had broken the mould in her family by electing to have a child in vitro, in her late 30's, rather than via traditional means in her late teens. When I met Tash, she was re-training to become a school teacher and was in the midst of rehabilitating a freak spinal injury, which required major surgery to fix months earlier. She had slowly progressed to the point where she could move around unassisted, but was not able to sit down for very long without pain. The three-piece suite that she now needed to part with, because it was taking up too much space in her house, was quite dear to her heart. It had served as the only place where she could sleep comfortably in the early days post-surgery. How she balanced her recovery with looking after a small child I don't know, but Tash's anecdote was a mark of quality unrivalled by any magazine's five-star review. I would have been a fool to say no.

My last recollection is possibly the most remarkable,

depending on whether you believe that the universe is governed by random insentient statistical events, which sentient humans then assign meaning to, or whether you believe that we do indeed have a destiny. I come from a small village in the West Country called Frampton Cotterell, which is 10 miles north of the city of Bristol. I travelled over 10,000 miles to a small Australian settlement called Sussex Inlet, where I met a classic car enthusiast called Douglas. Douglas came to Australia when he was eight years old, after growing up in the UK in the county of Dorset. From Douglas, I managed to buy a second-hand 1993 Mitsubishi Magna V6 TR Executive Sedan which had originally been bought, by Douglas, to serve the needs of an old friend from the UK who was no longer able to visit Australia due to COVID 19. This friend happened to live in the town of Yate. For the unfamiliar, Yate is a small town that is literally ten minutes up the road from Frampton Cotterell. What seems even more unlikely, is that the Magna was in immaculate condition despite having 300,000km on the clock. It had only had one owner (who was Swiss) for almost all of its life because it was a manual. Australians like automatics, but this made it perfect for Douglas because his friend was from the UK, and we drive manuals. What's even more unlikely still, is that even if Douglas's friend had made it to Australia, he wouldn't have been able to use the Magna because he had recently been involved in an accident that had cost him one of his legs. Ultimately, he would have needed an automatic which can be driven by unipeds.

I don't know if we each have a destiny or if we're all just floating around accidental like on a breeze, but I think I was meant to have that Magna. We was like peas and carrots.

XI

FIGHTING THE INEVITABLE

There's a reason that I was only in Shoalhaven for four months, even though it had taken me over two years of work to get there. Long story short, it slowly crystallised over that period of time that due to reasons beyond my control, my employer was unable to meet the internship requirements set down by AA. To give you some context, when overseas qualified Audiologists arrive in Australia, they have to complete a twelve-month internship before they are let off the leash so to speak. AA set the requirements for the internship, which are strict. I was subsequently relegated back to the starting blocks, where I began my search for an employer with a greater capacity for accommodating internships.

Now, I know what you might be thinking, because Tash brought the same thing to my attention after I emailed her the original manuscript for this chapter: *"why did you leave only after a few months? If people really knew why, it would make a lot more sense"*. I'll admit that I was torn when I first chronicled this part of the story; in 2022 I was much closer to what I still see as a fortunate escape from an intense welcome to country. I was subsequently needled by worries about what being specific, or pursuing further action, might mean for my employment prospects. History teaches us that being a whistle-blower doesn't make you desirable in the job market, and my financial position was more vulnerable at that time. I was also prognosticating worst case legal scenarios that could ignite, if the honourable retelling of past events were interpreted as being intentionally slanderous. However, now that alternative arrangements to see out the rest of my time in Oz have been secured, the benefits of sharing an unpleasant experience as a warning to immigrating Audiologists of the future, who might face comparable circumstances upon their arrival into country, is a philanthropic argument that I find harder to resist with every passing day.

Nevertheless, we will tread lightly and carry a big stick by heeding the advice of Agatha Christie's retired judge, Mr. Justice Wargrave, who once wisely proclaimed: *"you are assuming hearsay to be evidence; that may have been a false statement. There can be no exceptions allowed on the score of character, position, or probability. What me must now examine is the possibility of eliminating one or more persons on the facts."* Therefore, what follows is a plain chronological presentation of purposefully anonymised email correspondences, which transpired between May and August 2021. The attachments that are referenced in these emails, which I utilised at the time to objectively support my subjective grievances, are retained to this day for safekeeping. You never know.

16/5/2021

Me: Dear Fair Work Australia. I am an Audiologist currently working in NSW. I came to Australia on a TSS 482 VISA, and have been working here since the 7th of April 2021. My understanding is that you are the acting Fair Trades Ombudsman and are, therefore, an expert in matters of employee fair pay. I hope that you or one of your team can guide me on my rights in my current position. I have attached my current employment contract and my current VISA for your reference, in addition to my current history of logged working hours. Audiologists are contracted to work 8:45am - 5:15pm Monday to Friday. I only started work recently, and am still learning how to operate under the rules of an Australian healthcare system, which is quite different to the UK healthcare system. The preferred method of clinical supervision comes in the form of weekly case study reviews. I am expected to keep all of the paper notes for patients I have seen, in a drawer, and then present them to my supervisor chronologically; to figure out whether I have done the work correctly. Due to an absence of direct supervision at the moment I usually find that I have made errors, which, after they had been pointed out, I am required to stay late and remedy. Our case study discussions tend to be several days apart so remedying the mistakes, for the volume of patients that I had seen during this time period, takes significant time.

Since starting work I have: turned up an hour early, worked through lunch, and stayed an hour late on average to keep on top of my patient load. I am not paid overtime for this. I have digitally clocked my total working hours, using the app provided, to support this statement. I have attached a word document for your reference which highlights all of the hours that I have worked thus far.

Do I have a right to be paid overtime for these extra hours?

19/5/2021

Fair Work Ombudsman: I am writing in response to your email to Fair Work Ombudsman, dated 16 May 2021. I would like to discuss your situation with you. Could you please advise an appropriate contact number and suitable time for me to call you?

Me: Thank you for getting back to me. As you imagine, having conversations of this nature while I am in a confined office space with my current employer, would be awkward. I can sometimes step out of the building at lunchtime for a private conversation, or early morning/after 5:15pm. Do you have any scope to accommodate me outside usual 9-5? Sorry to be an inflexible nuisance.

Fair Work Ombudsman: Fortunately, I start work at around 7:30am each day. I will call you around 8am tomorrow morning.

Me: I will have a half hour window before anyone else arrives, between 8-8:30am. I hope that's enough.

Fair Work Ombudsman: If we can call you before 8 we will, but half an hour should be sufficient.

20/5/2021

Fair Work Ombudsman: Thanks for sending the payslip. This payslip shows a gross payment for the fortnight. As advised during our telephone conversation, this payment would be sufficient to cover approximately 8 hours overtime per week, assuming the overtime is worked in blocks of up to 2 hours per time. As agreed during our conversation, FWO will take no further action with regard to your situation. I understand that you will monitor and keep a record of your work patterns going forward, being aware that you can lodge a request for assistance with us at any time up to 6 years after a contravention of your entitlements occurring.

16/5/2021 (email to Audiology Australia)

Me: Dear AA. I write this email to you with a heavy heart, and I would ask that you please treat everything that I am about to confide in you as completely confidential. I feel like I am in a very sensitive situation at present, and for the sake of maintaining an already tense work environment, please do not share this with my supervisor. I officially landed in Sydney on the 22nd of March, although I was advised to register for the AA internship in January, by my supervisor, before I left the UK. In hopes that she would be able to fast track the internship process, due to my 5 years of UK clinical experience, upon my eventual arrival which was delayed due to COVID19. I am officially registered as starting the internship on 18th of January 2021, but I didn't start work until the 7th of April 2021.

Having read your internship handbook, I was expecting to be 100% directly supervised during my first 6 weeks. Defined as: *The supervisor must directly observe the intern during their practice and be physically present at all times, i.e., 100% of consultations. The intern must consult with the supervisor and follow directions from the supervisor regarding the management of each client before care is delivered.* The former part of this definition did not come to fruition. Within a few days, I was being expected to autonomously manage my clinics and see patients unsupervised. I found this very nerve-wracking and uncomfortable. Despite my past clinical experiences, the NHS and the Australian voucher program is not interchangeable, and there is a great deal to learn about how it works, and how its rules should be applied correctly. All of this was occurring during a period where I was attempting to find a place to live, open up a bank account, acquire a Medicare card and tax file number (to legally receive my salary), open a superannuation fund, and acquire an Australian phone number. There have been two Fridays where I was the only Audiologist on-site, supported by one receptionist. Friday the 14th was the most recent example of this.

The preferred method of supervision, comes in the form of weekly case study reviews. I was expected to keep all of the paper notes of patients I had seen, in a drawer, and then present them chronologically in order to figure out whether I had done the work correctly. Often, I had made errors, which after they had been pointed out to me, I would be required to stay late and remedy them. Our case study discussions tended to be several days apart, so remedying the mistakes for the volume of patients that I had seen during this time period, after hours, took significant time.

Furthermore, my case study sessions thus far have proven to be a very uncomfortable experience, I have lost a lot of confidence in my abilities since starting here. The work environment feels claustrophobic; I am learning that two staff members are currently interviewing elsewhere, and the new receptionist who started here in March has already handed in her notice. The honest revelations I have confided in you here have the potential to make an already tense workspace, much more unpleasant. I do not wish to be made redundant on the grounds of perceived insubordination. This is why I wish for you not to make any investigations, that you may wish to make, public outside of the AA until I have resigned. I am currently in the process of contacting other employers, in the hopes of securing alternative employment, and potentially continuing on the rest of my internship with them. I would be grateful for any advice and support that you and the AA can offer me. Thank you for taking the time to read this, and I look forward to hearing from you.

17/5/21

Audiology Australia: Thank you for your email. I can assure you that this matter will be dealt with confidentially. Is there a time when I can have a quick chat to you over the phone? Alternatively, you can call me.

Me: I tried to give you a call just a couple of minutes ago, I have to step out to call you because it's too close proximity to answer the phone during the day and speak freely. I have a lunch break until 1:30pm. Are you back at your desk? I will try again before I go back in?

17/5/21 (Post AA Phone Call)

Me: I have some further information for you, which should aid your enquiries. I have attached an email conversation that I had with my supervisor before I arrived in Oz, on March 22nd. I have highlighted all chat surrounding the premature start of the clinical internship program before I arrived, and my concerns about this at the time. I have included a scanned copy of my boarding pass, and Sydney quarantine paperwork, to prove my official date of arrival in Australia. On some dates, you wanted to know when direct supervision stopped. I started work on Wednesday the 7th of April. The 7th was an induction day, the 8th and the 9th I was supervised in the clinic. On the 13th of April, I began working autonomously without supervision, and retrospective case reviews became the norm for assessing my progress. It has been this way ever since.

My supervisor is currently booked to go away on annual leave on the 25th of May, and will be gone for several weeks until the end of June, I believe. I have agreed to this because her absence will actually provide me with some breathing room to keep finding alternative employment. I do not yet know her plans for remote supervision during this period. You also asked what can the AA do for me. In addition to any advice about how overseas candidates have resolved similar issues in the past. As I continue to seek new employment, and if you side in my favour, would I be able to get an official AA letter of support to reassure employers that I am not simply a job hopper, and had legitimate reasons to break my current employment contract?

18/5/21

Audiology Australia: Thank you for your email. I have had a meeting internally and confidentially to discuss your case. It has been advised that as a first step it would be best for you to contact the Ethics Officer to get advice. Please note that if we raise this issue with your supervisor, then it will require some involvement from your end and as you've indicated, you may not want to do this as long as you are employed at this place. So as a first step, please contact the Ethics Officer. Please let me know how you go and if there's anything else I can assist you with, then please don't hesitate to contact me.

    Me: Thank you for not forgetting about me and following this through. I will contact the ethics officer and see what she has to say. I am still in the process of finding an alternative employer, and if any action is going to be taken it would be better for me to be clear first. I do not want other emigrants to fall into the same trap, but I also do not want repercussions that may come from a formal investigation sullying my future. Whistle-blowers traditionally do not do well in the job market. I will keep you informed as best I can. Wish me luck because I will need it.

26/6/21

Me: I have an update for you. I have now successfully acquired new employment and I will be based at their Rockhampton clinic. I am due to start in Rockhampton on the 16th of August and will be making preparations to hand in my letter of resignation, break my current rental lease, and make the move up to Queensland in the coming days. My supervisor has been in a predominantly uncontactable location on annual leave since the end of May, and she is not due to return to work until the 19th of July. I am not intending to hand in my written notice as per my contractual obligations until then, but I am preparing for my last day to be on the 30th of July. I have yet to meet all the members of the Rockhampton team; introductions are due to take place on the 5th and 6th of August in Brisbane. Would you please advise me as to what steps need to be taken to successfully transfer my internship?

1/7/21

AA: That's great news. Congratulations on your new job offer. When you start on 16th August, please click on 'change supervisor' on your internship portal and add the details of your new employer. On receiving this, we'll reset the end date of your internship and advice you of the dates of the quarterly submissions. The record of your current internship will also be saved on your file for future reference.

7/7/21 (email to supervisor)

Me: Apologies that you are receiving this via email under the current circumstances, arguably there was never going to be a good time to deliver this news. I have accepted a competitive job offer in Queensland, and intend to resign at the end of July. Please find my formal letter of resignation attached to this email, along with my contract and financial obligations for reference. I will await your instruction, concerning how you would like to proceed, in the coming days.

24/7/21 (email to AA)

Me: I had my resignation conversation yesterday afternoon, and it was an uncomfortable affair. In response to my resignation, my supervisor has taken the verbal stance that I have been a burden to the clinic and wishes me to financially reimburse her for the cost of my original VISA application. I am currently formulating my defence with the fair work ombudsman and the department of home affairs. I wanted to warn you that she has many questions about my idea of what an AA internship should be. I have directed her towards the definitions, about the rules of the AA internship, that are written down in the internship handbook. I have also made her aware that when we spoke on the 17th of May, you informed me that the official start date of my internship should not have been initialised on the 18/01/2021, because I had not entered the country. It should have started on 7/4/21, which is when I actually started work. I also explained that regardless of my past experience in the UK, I was entitled to the same internship as Australian graduates. Please would you confirm that this is definitely still the AA's stance? My supervisor appeared very unhappy with my descriptions and felt that these were unreasonable requirements. I did not feel that it was my place to defend the reasoning behind the AA internship regulations, so I have encouraged her to speak to you directly about this. She may be in touch and I thought you would appreciate a heads up.

26/7/2021

AA: Thank you for your email and I am sorry to hear about these challenges you are facing. As per the internship policy, the duration is 12 months and the definition for different types of supervision and the minimum supervision requirements are all clearly defined in the policy. If an intern is seeking to receive reduction in the total internship duration, then a written application along with supporting documents have to be submitted for assessment. This is usually the case where the intern has already completed significant amount of supervision with another Audiology Australia accredited audiologist at another professional body. All applications are assessed on a case-by-case basis. Unless prior approval is sought, the internship duration is 12 months. I hope this clarifies. Please let me know if we can assist you with anything.

24/7/21 (email to Fair Work Ombudsman)

Me: I hope you are well. I have now formally resigned and my last day is on the 28th of July. I have secured alternative employment in Rockhampton, which is due to start on the 16th of August. Audiology Australia has agreed to reset my internship program upon commencement in my new role, in acknowledgement that their conditions have not been met on this occasion. I had my formal resignation meeting with my supervisor yesterday afternoon, and it was not a pleasant experience. Talks went on for 45 minutes, and the stance that she has decided to take is that I am a burden to her clinic and because I have only worked for 3 months, rather than for the entire 4-year length of my TSS 482 VISA, she wants me to reimburse her the sum of $5,130. The details of this calculation were not provided.

She produced a document during the meeting outlining an intention to sacrifice my final pay to satisfy her proposed reimbursement, and she is currently withholding my salary to date. I should have been paid for the last two weeks on the 22nd of July. So far, I have received nothing, and I have also not received my PAYG tax summary. My last successful payday was the 8th of July; we are meant to be paid fortnightly. I want to state for the record that yesterday was the first time that I had seen this document, and I had no part in writing it. I do not intend to sign this document, nor have I verbally agreed to it. I informed her that I would be pursuing independent advice in this matter instead.

She did not permit me to take a copy of the proposed agreement, composed in my name, but I did manage to take a photograph of it before the meeting came to an end. There is nothing written in my contract tying me for the entire 4 years of my VISA, and I am also of the understanding that asking employees to reimburse employers for the costs of a VISA application is illegal, based on my conversations with the department of home affairs.

Please would you provide me with your guidance and support in this matter. I have attached all relevant documentation as evidence for your consideration, and will assist you in your enquiries as best I can.

Attached are the following documents:

• The picture that I captured of the proposed salary sacrifice arrangement to reimburse the VISA costs (I have not agreed to this)

- The document highlighting the proposed amount that my supervisor wants me to pay back, to compensate for the costs of the VISA
- Screenshots of my work hours, digitally clocked using the smartphone app provided, which I have not been paid for to date (from the 9th of July to the present day)
- My employment contracts
- Screenshot of my Commonwealth bank account to demonstrate the absence of salary payment due on 22nd of July, which has not been paid
- My TSS 482 VISA

I await your advice.

Fair Work Ombudsman: It is correct that a sponsor cannot recover visa nomination costs from a sponsored visa holder. However, the visa costs are those of the visa holder and, in certain circumstances, may be recovered if the sponsor has paid them on behalf of the visa holder. For this to occur, however, there would need to be an authority to deduct, signed by the visa holder. It would appear that this is the document your sponsor has asked you to sign. As you have not authorised a salary deduction to cover these costs, withholding of your entitlements is a contravention of the Fair Work Act. I would advise a further conversation with your sponsor, advising them that you have sought our advice regarding withholding of your entitlements. If this is unsuccessful in resolving the issue, we can assist. If you need our assistance in this matter, please confirm by return email and we will lodge a Request for Assistance on your behalf and commence an investigation. You should note that, if the sponsor regards the costs as a valid debt, they may seek to recover them from you by other means. I am unable to provide guidance on this – you would need to seek independent legal advice.

[Which I did…more on that later]

27/7/2021

Me: I have emailed my supervisor, and let her know that I have sought your advice. In response to this, she has now released the salary that was originally due last Thursday. I also infer from her response that she is not going to pursue me for any VISA nomination and sponsorship acquisition costs anymore. When I leave tomorrow, the only outstanding payment would be my final pay package. Would you confirm what should be included in that package, and when it should be paid, please? Am I right in thinking it should include all days worked from last Thursday, accrued annual leave and superannuation?

Fair Work Ombudsman: That's good news. Your final payment should include salary for days worked since your last pay and your accrued annual leave entitlement. Superannuation should be paid to your nominated superannuation fund. Payment should be made immediately but allowance may need to be made for pay cycles i.e., the next scheduled pay day after you finish work would be acceptable. You should receive a final pay slip detailing these payments within one day of the payment being made.

Me: Thank you for taking the time. Hopefully you won't need to hear from me again; I will be back in touch if I have difficulty securing my final pay.

2/8/2021 (email to supervisor)

Me: My final pay did not show up in my account today as

expected. Was there a problem with the processing? The payment that was released to my account, and received on the 26th, was payment in arrears for the previous 2 weeks that I had worked. The outstanding money which I am referring to here, that I have not yet received, are my final pay entitlements as laid out by the fair work ombudsman.

• outstanding wages for hours they have worked, including penalty rates and allowances

• any accumulated annual leave, including annual leave loading if it would have been paid during employment

By my count, my outstanding hours would be for the: 23rd, 26th, 27th, and 28th of July, in addition to my accumulated annual leave. Would you give me an indication as to when my final pay package will be sent, please.

Supervisor: Thanks for alerting me to the non-arrival of your final pay. I have rectified the problem with processing and resent the pay. Please let me know if you do not receive it.

3/8/2021

Me: I can confirm that my final pay has now been received. Thank you for sorting.

Supervisor: Thank you!

And there you have it. That's how two extraordinary years' worth of correspondence, and any semblance of a working relationship with my supervisor, came to an end. When the Fair Work Ombudsman advised that I might need to seek independent legal advice, I reached out to the CEO of my new employer in Rockhampton for help, who subsequently gave me the contact details of a trusted lawyer who specialised in workplace relations.

I vividly remember the conversation that I had with this lawyer, because my smartphone rang half-way through my morning clinic. Unable to step out, I suddenly found myself recreating the same paranoia of being overheard, which Robert Redford portrayed in the iconic deepthroat scenes from the film: *All the President's Men*. Panic defeated composure for the control of my actions, inspiring me to dive straight into the nearest sound booth, where I locked the door behind me. The obvious flaw in my plan was that this booth was not windowless; it would have looked very suspicious to anybody who might have chosen to walk in at that moment, to see me locked inside my own testing chamber deep in conversation. The main message that the lawyer impressed upon me, during our soundproof consultation that morning, echoes in my mind to this day: *"just because something is against the rules, doesn't necessarily mean that businesses won't try breaking them anyway"*. I would implore all aspiring immigrants reading this to remember this sombre statement; it was delivered directly from the voice of experience.

On my last day in clinic, I handed back my keys to the shit-box on wheels, and began my long walk home. Tracy had also resigned by then, and she was kind enough to offer me a lift home in her car. It was a 90-minute walk after all.

After interviewing with three different employers, all of whom started their interview with the question: *"So... how did you get here exactly?"* I was offered a new job in Rockhampton; which is an eighteen hour drive north of Shoalhaven in the state of Queensland. After being offered the position, I was due to start in August 2021. This was bittersweet news, because it meant that after only four months in Australia I was already facing the prospect of: getting rid of almost all the stuff that I had just recently acquired (turns out that if you put it on the pavement, it

78

disappears like magic), paying the financial penalty of breaking my rental lease early, packing up the Magna, and saying goodbye to the people I had gotten to know in Sanctuary Point. Frankly, I was exhausted. What I didn't realise at the time, was just how much of an epic saga my journey to Rockhampton would turn out to be. From the time the COVID 19 pandemic began, Australia had been a near-impenetrable fortress protected by its travel ban. However, by June 2021 the COVID 19 Delta variant, which had already ravaged India by then, was about to kick the door in and flip the script with a ferocity that Australia was not prepared for.

While the Delta variant was infecting Sydney, and slowly creeping further south, my rental lease in Sanctuary Point was about to end; rendering me homeless in the process. I had resigned from my job which meant I had no salary. Rockhampton, the place that I needed to be in order to reach my new home, and start my new job, was an eighteen hour drive away in a state that was about to protect itself by imposing impermeable border restrictions with: NSW, Victoria, and South Australia, which were set to last until further notice. To borrow a quote from the glorious Gloucestershire Regiment Brigadier, Thomas Brodie, when he was facing overwhelming odds in the bloody Battle of the Imjin River, during the Korean War, my situation was: *"a bit sticky, things are pretty sticky down there"*.

Now you wouldn't believe me if I told you, but after a month of living on the road I did eventually arrive in Rockhampton, after escaping the NSW red zone and the Delta variant. But that is another story.

XII

THE BALLAD OF TRACY & MARTY

To understand how I managed to evade the Delta strain, and escape from the New South Wales (NSW) red zone, you must appreciate that I am indebted to Tracy and Marty. They were the two people who convinced me that everything was going to be all right, and that there was hope on the horizon. I met Tracy first because she was there on my first day at work, which is where I learned that we had something in common. All of her family and friends were back in Sydney and Newcastle, so even though she was a native Australian we were both essentially blow ins to the local area, beginning again. She had moved down to Sanctuary Point to be with Marty, who did have a family connection. As the days went by, Tracy and I charmed the habit of checking in with each other before clinic began, bonding over the challenges of being the new kids on the block.

Even though Tracy had never left Australia (unless you count Tasmania, which you shouldn't), she was very much a person of the world. She began her life in Queensland (QLD) before moving to NSW and in addition to running her own radio show in Blacktown, with her friend Greggo, she had worked at the desk of a famous Sydney brothel as a teenager. She had been responsible for checking in the male clients and keeping them comfortable, whilst the rich portfolio of ladies prepared themselves to enact the girlfriend experience. Tracy adored:

80

karaoke, cigarettes, and the prospect of marriage. In fact, Tracy had been married and divorced four times before she met Marty, which had not discouraged her in the slightest. Tracy liked to be charmed by authenticity; so when the military man who would become husband number two approached her in a bar to offer a glass of bourbon, which she politely refused because she doesn't drink bourbon, he had responded with: *"fuck you then"* and walked away. She had her friend give him her number later that night, and the rest is history. As fate would have it, said friend would later become husband number three.

Tracy was a master of disguise and had taken care to fully commit to a completely different theme, every time she had walked down the aisle. Quite successfully I might add based on the wedding photos I have seen, Mystique eat your heart out. As time went by I got to meet some of Tracy's family when they came to visit. Her youngest son was a pharmaceutically informed tea smoker, and he blew my mind the first time I met him when he explained to me that the sound your fingers make when you click, is attributable to the moment that your finger hits your palm and not the friction caused by the finger and thumb rubbing together.

Tracy lived with ADHD, and used medicine to manage her anxiety as best she could. She is still to this day the only person I know who doesn't like the film Team America World Police, because she found the shimmery micro-movements of the puppets to be too stimulating. Tracy also dispelled the myth that Gynaecologists are good lovers, after having dated one herself and found him to be only average in bed (she also has one of the funniest tampon anecdotes that I have ever heard which solidified my suspicion that all men, even the most well versed, will never really know everything the female vagina is capable of). Tracy

81

had an appalling memory, but she compensated for this with pure heart. When she deduced that I was in the process of acquiring furniture she very kindly offered me the use of Marty's trailer; knowing full well that a three-piece suite was too large for the Daihatsu. This is how I came to meet the man himself.

Tracy describes Marty as a star waiting to be discovered. Marty would say that he is glad to be a source of maximum entertainment. He was originally a mechanic by trade, but quickly moved into automotive workshop equipment sales for a Melbourne based company. His work had taken him all over Australia and he seemed to have a story about every small town you can think of, apart from Broome and Seventeen Seventy that is. Those two had eluded his collection much to his chagrin. I was immediately struck by his effortlessly casual righto philosophy. After shaking my hand, and hooking up the trailer, we drove off into the night as a lightning storm threatened. We were bound for a gated community, around St George's Basin, where Tash was waiting for us. This is where we both discovered that her gated community happened to be protected by a gate control panel stuck on Spanish. No problem for Marty and his righto philosophy. Not discouraged by the fact that he was not a Spanish speaker himself, he simply leaned out of the window and started pressing buttons until the gate opened, which it did, and in we went. I'm always very aware of people's legal rights in situations like this. When Tracy had mentioned to him that she had met a pom called Tom, who needed help acquiring some furniture, he would have been completely within his rights to say: *"why's that my problem?"*.

Marty didn't owe me anything and we weren't related, and yet, here he was helping a complete stranger to load heavy furniture into the trailer, and debating whether straps would be needed to keep it from getting damaged as we bounced home. Furthermore, he seemed to be putting in the effort in good spirits, and not at all begrudgingly, despite the fact that his evening was his own and he could have been sat on his sofa enjoying a stubby. After that night, Tracy and Marty invited me over to their place on several occasions, and I came to relish my time spent with them. Not least because they spoiled me with Australian barbecue, and Marty's signature spaghetti Bolognese, which was delicious. As I got to know him better, I began to understand why Tracy had described him as a star waiting to be discovered.

Marty's parents originally lived in Sydney and his Dad had worked alongside Les Chadwick, who was the bass guitar player in the band Gerry and the Pacemakers, after Les had immigrated to Sydney from Liverpool. There's mischief in their blood. Marty and his sister are currently locked into an ongoing game of clown smuggling; their family have a picture of a terrifying clown, which they got for Christmas one year, and the game is to give it to the other person as a gift without them realising until they open it. Whoever opens the gift without realising has to keep it until the next gift giving opportunity. Marty is very proud of the fact that he has been banned from Facebook (and let back in he hastens to add), over thirty times, for sharing what was deemed to be explicitly sexual jokes through messenger with his friends: *"I'm just talking about things that are real"* he would say in his defence, and: *"what's thirty minutes between friends"*.

During his time living in Sydney, Marty managed to qualify in the top ten for a city wide amateur stand-up competition. He is also able to count the then Miss Newcastle amongst his various sexual conquests. Marty will tell you that he pulled this off because he happened to be the tallest person in the club that she was attending that night, but all those who have met him will know that he has kissed the proverbial blarney stone; it was his gift of the gab which no doubt helped him on his way. Marty was a mechanic for five years in the garages on the streets of Sydney, where he discovered that Sydneysider mechanics liked to the say the F word, a lot. F this and F that. When he wasn't turning the air blue at work, Marty would spend time in the company of friends. One of whom was called Scrote, and he had a nefarious gift. Scrote would crash hen parties at city night clubs, and would then make it his mission to see whether he could pull the bride to be. Marty informs me that by the time he was eighteen years old Scrote already had a fifty per cent success rate.

Then there was Luke, the New Zealand farmer, who cemented his place in Marty's heart when he gave him a place to stay during his divorce. Luke had a growth in his nose, that could not be removed surgically, which rendered him unable to taste anything. He was renowned for being able to handle the hottest curry on offer anywhere he went. Marty was once partially responsible for subjecting this guy to an extraordinarily hot chilli that required gloves to handle for safety reasons, and really only required a miniscule dab to provide a volcanic experience. When they had lived together, Marty had been to an agricultural show in QLD and had brought back this deadly chilli for Luke to try. Without warning, Luke decided to paste the entire sample all over his pizza and ate the lot. Marty saw Luke the next morning in a sweat, saying that he didn't feel good. In fact, Luke had convulsed and vomited everything he had eaten during the night while he was high on marijuana. It took him a day and a half to recover.

On another occasion, when Luke was making a delivery, he had managed to sweet-talk his way into the affections of a

Brazilian lady at the local bank. Unfortunately, this very attractive Brazilian lady that Luke had his eyes on, got the wrong idea and offered him the hand of her less debonair sister whom she thought would be perfect for him. Not to be unkind, Luke agreed and she moved in not long after. A couple of weeks went by before Luke took Marty aside to confess his true feelings: "we have to get rid of her mate, she ate your last cherry tomato". "How are we gonna do it?" Marty agreed, and Luke eventually replied "Well let's tell her that we got evicted". Luke is not a good liar, so Marty coached him through it: "Right, tell her we got evicted, so you're gonna have to go back to your ex-wife's place. And you can't have her coming around as a new Brazilian girlfriend in the picture because it won't work, and Marty is gonna go back to his ex-wife's place and take it from there". Somehow she bought it, and so goes the tale of Marty and Luke's friendship, they remain thick as thieves.

Underneath the: frat boy tomfoolery, irreverence, and the innate desire to never take life too seriously, Marty was undeniably a man of heart. His family were originally from Latvia, and his grandmother had always expressed a desire for her ashes to be returned home after she died. After the funeral, Marty collected his grandmother's ashes and planned on taking her to Latvia during a work trip to Italy; which was coming up in the near future. He figured that he could extend his work trip and take some time to see the rest of Europe, but there was an unforeseen problem. It's illegal in Italy to: scatter, bury, or transfer human remains. Catholics as a general rule don't favour cremation because they prefer to honour the tradition of burying their dead, in the same way that Jesus Christ was buried after his crucifixion. This meant that if Marty was going to fulfil his grandmother's wishes, he was going to have to smuggle her through Italy to get her to Latvia. Not to be discouraged at the prospect of angry Catholics and breaking the law, to do what was right, he sought counsel from a mate who told him: *"put the ashes in your toiletry bag and say its medication. Nobody will ever check inside the wash bag if you say that"*. And they never did. So, Marty drove his grandmother to Riga, the Latvian capital, and laid her to rest as promised in the Daugava River.

Marty met Tracy in Sydney years later, after she had separated from husband number four. Marty's parents had retired down to Sanctuary Point by then, but when his Dad died his mother moved back to Sydney, and the children inherited the house. In order to directly oversee the development of the premises Marty moved down to Sanctuary Point with Tracy, not months before I arrived myself, and the rest is history. Not that any of us knew it when the universe first threw us together, but they were to be the key to my escape.

XIII

IT'S NOT WHAT YOU KNOW, IT'S WHO YOU KNOW

As it became clear that my current employer wasn't in a position to satisfy the internship requirements of Audiology Australia (AA), as previously sold, I was faced with the prospect of abandoning that which I had worked two years to obtain to find a new job with a larger employer, after having only worked in my current position for four months, which on paper tends to shout: 'job hopper'. I also needed to lose any furniture that I couldn't fit into the Mitsubishi Magna. It was different this time because now I was starting again without a safety net. My family support system was now 10,000 miles away, and if I didn't find a new job quickly enough this would break the conditions of my work VISA, and I would be sent home. Enter Tracy and Marty. Their gravitational pull was strong when it came to making new friends, and they introduced me to some critical people. One such friend was an Amazonian twin called Donna, who was quite literally larger than life.

To paint you a picture; standing over 6 feet with the body of a powerlifter, when I met Donna, she was wearing black prison guard shoes and sported a tattoo of a date, with unknown significance, on her left ankle. Her hair was in a tight pony tail and her eyebrows had been tweezed which accentuated her steely gaze. It would be a misnomer to say that Donna was one of a kind, because she had a twin sister called Diane. Tracy had met

Donna ('Donzie' to her friends) during her time working for Bay Audio as a client advocate. It was Donna's job to stand outside the shop, and coax new customers inside as they passed. From what Marty tells me, after being on the receiving end, Donna made offers that were hard to refuse. I'm told that Donna would do anything for you, but she was not a woman that you would ever want as an enemy. I believed this conclusion all the more after I heard some of her anecdotes. She had once put a duck in a headlock after it had flown into her face to protect its ducklings, and had a fight with a one-eyed possum. Furthermore, Donna had once inflicted rough justice upon a woman in a toilet cubicle, at a birthday party, with her sister after they had discovered that she had been stealing wallets. Donna's finest hour however, had come when she foiled an armed robbery single handed.

The Returned and Services League of *Australia* (*RSL*) club, near to where Donna used to live, was once the victim of a robbery. Word had spread that they were keeping at least $5000 in the safe. Two men entered the club one night armed with a sawn-off shotgun and a baseball bat. Hearing the commotion, some of the staff managed to take refuge in a locked room which unfortunately was the very place that the robbers were attempting to break into, because that was where the safe was. The two men began breaking down the door. Among the trapped employees was Donna's husband, who found enough time to call her and sound the alarm before he was taken hostage. Donna jumped out of bed, put on her pink dressing gown and slippers, roused her son, and off they went to the RSL. She stopped in at the police station en-route to report what was occurring, but nobody was there. So, she gets back in her car and continues on to the RSL, only to find the local police officer and the assistant manager of the RSL club, *"pissed as a nit"*, in the pub across the road. *"Donna what's going on here?"* the officer had said *"the RSL is being robbed"* Donna replied as she stood there in her dressing gown, readying herself to enter the building and rescue her husband. At that moment she heard the chug of a boat engine starting up on the jetty, which signalled the robbers making their escape.

At this point, Donna noticed something that the inebriated police officer did not. It was at this moment that the assistant manager went storming into the building without arming himself first. *"That's not something that any ordinary person would do, unless they knew that they wouldn't come to harm"* Donna had thought to herself, and she was right. She let the police know about her suspicions later that week. It turns out that the assistant manager had been seen moving the cameras in the RSL club to all face in different directions, earlier that week, in preparation for the robber's entry. Not content with catching the brains of the operation, Donna eventually identified one of the two robbers as well when he visited her workplace one day quite by happenstance. One of the robbers had entered the shop where Donna was working as a stocktake.

This was an unusual job for Donna, because those that know her best will tell you that she must not be trusted with computers. The suspicious looking man had accidentally dropped his driving license on the floor, which was subsequently handed in by another patron. Donna's friend showed the license to her, reporting that something about this man had given her 'bad vibes' while he was browsing in the shop. A lightbulb went off in Donna's mind and she decided to photocopy the license on a hunch, and subsequently send the details through to police. The man did have a past criminal record and after police tracked him down they were eventually able to link him, and his friend, to the robbery. The police officer who handled the case reportedly said to Donna: *"I'm glad you didn't manage to get in there that night Donna, because you probably would have killed someone."*

Fortuitously enough, in addition to entertaining characters like Donna who wouldn't be out of place in either a Guy Ritchie film or an Agatha Christie novel, Tracy also had connections in the non-stop world of job acquisition. One of the many past lives that Tracy had lived was as a healthcare recruitment consultant, and she was still friendly with several people that she used to work with. One of whom was now a managing director, called Matt, who was known affectionately to his friends as Thumb; owing to the fact that his head was perfectly glabrous. Like me, Matt was not Australian. He actually came from Cornwall originally but he had taken care to lose his Cornish brogue so that he would be taken seriously by his colleagues in London, after he moved there to seek his fortune in the recruitment industry. He met Tracy after migrating to Australia, and after becoming jaded at what he saw as the immorality of mainstream recruitment consultancy, he left to start his own business. Matt was what can only be described as good people, and he was only too happy to help me as part of his ongoing fight for justice in the world. Matt put me in touch with one of the best audiology recruiters in the business, and I suddenly found myself with a baton to run with.

Marty by comparison had lucrative connections closer to home. To satisfy the requirements of my tenancy agreement I needed to put the property back into a sterile and empty state, which meant that all the furniture had to go. Marty had been eyeing up Tash's three-piece suite since the day he had helped me transport it. I was all too happy to give it to him. Marty had come with me to see Douglas on the day I went to buy the Magna, to help me judge whether it was in good enough condition to purchase. His mechanical expertise has been worth its weight in gold, because that car hasn't failed me yet. He also helped me to do a full service on it before I left Sanctuary Point, so in my mind he had easily earned a comfortable sofa. Particularly when you consider how much his time would have cost me in a commercial setting. Furthermore, he was willing to come and collect the furniture, which was a weight off my mind and also my wallet. Marty was an aspiring captain (of a motorboat called Jinxy) and he had taken care to make friends with a retired boatman who, in addition to baking mind-expanding cookies that put Amsterdam to shame, was looking to sell his old fishing vessel. In response to the news that I needed to get rid of my second-hand top loader washing machine and fridge, Marty had brokered a deal with old matey boy on my behalf. Just like that, I had new homes for my largest household items. It really is who you know that matters. Everything else from manual lawn mowers to step ladders, which were all too big to pack into the Magna, either went into the local skip or on to the street where they disappeared like magic.

When I consider how much money it would have cost to acquire the services that Tracy and Marty selflessly gave me for free, in the weeks before I left Sanctuary Point, I would probably have had to spend hundreds or thousands of dollars. They would have none of it but I did insist on buying them a leaving gift to say thank you, in the form of a mega pack of Woodstock Bourbon and Cola. It really speaks to their character when they told me that even this was too much. It really wasn't.

91

XIV

DON'T WORRY THE BRITISH EMBASSY WILL SAVE US

After fully exploiting Tracy and Matt's recruitment connections, I was eventually offered jobs by three different employers in three different locations: one in Darwin, one in Cairns, and another in Rockhampton. After much deliberation, I took the job in Rockhampton and formally signed the contract on the 27th of June with a start date of the 16th of August. I tendered my resignation in Shoalhaven, on the 7th of July, giving my employer twenty-one days' notice that my final day would be on the 28th of July. I formally terminated my tenancy on the 15th of July, and my final day in the property was set for the 2nd of August. The scene was set for my exodus but problems were brewing in the Emerald City.

The third wave began with a limousine driver in his 60's; who was ferrying international airline crews from Sydney Airport to their quarantine hotel rooms, who came in contact with the coronavirus. He had not been vaccinated and on June 16th he tested positive for the Delta variant, which had only been recorded in India until that point in time. Delta is highly transmissible, and within a few hours his wife had also tested positive. Unfortunately, before he had become symptomatic patient zero had visited a busy shopping centre within walking distance of Bondi Beach, and the rest is history. Delta went on to become the dominant variant of COVID that infected what was a predominantly unvaccinated continent.

Australia's culture capital went the same way after a suspected hotel quarantine leak. Victorian Chief Health Officer Brett Sutton confirmed in early June that the Delta variant had been identified in a coronavirus test result. Genomic sequencing had confirmed the presence of Delta originating from a Sri-Lankan man who had entered Melbourne quarantine on 8/5/21. Not long after this revelation two members of a west Melbourne family, who visited NSW in May before testing positive for COVID-19, were also found to have the Delta variant. Several days after this, health authorities confirmed another case of the variant after examining the genomic sequence of a sample taken from a family of four, who had also travelled to NSW in May. Unfortunately, they had also visited rural communities in Goulburn and Jervis Bay on their travels, before becoming symptomatic and getting tested. Where they went the virus followed.

By Friday the 25th of June, health officials conceded the need to place Sydney into lockdown. By the 29th of June: Darwin, Perth, and Brisbane – all state capital cities – along with eighty per cent of Australia's entire population, were all living under restrictions. At 6pm on Tuesday 20 July 2021, a lockdown was imposed on South Australia too. For Melbourne, the Delta strain came after a long series of lockdowns which had plagued the city on and off since March, as they continued to wrestle with cluster outbreaks. I still remember how deflated I felt when I heard the news that all of **NSW,** at one a.m. on Friday 23rd July, would be considered a red zone by the QLD government. I received a call from Rockhampton not long after the news broke to reassure me that they understood the predicament I was in, and they would be flexible with regards to my start date.

I still had my job, that was something at least, but I was now faced with the unenviable challenge of trying to find a way to legally enter QLD. I thought I would start by submitting an application for a quarantine exemption, which could only be granted at that time by the then acting Chief Health Officer of QLD, Dr Jeannette Young. This is the covering letter that I was asked to submit to Dr Young; to justify my reason for applying to enter QLD without quarantining. I submitted this on the 22nd of July:

Dear Dr Jeanette Young (Chief QLD Health Officer),

My job as an Audiologist, in rural NSW, is due to come to an end on the 28th of July, my rental lease in Sanctuary Point is terminating on the 2nd of August.

I have been employed to provide essential: Adult, Paediatric, Cochlear Implant, and Vestibular services in Rockhampton Queensland. My new job is due to begin on the 16th of August, and my new rental lease is due to begin on the 11th of August. I need to travel to Queensland in order to provide these essential services to the hearing-impaired residents of Rockhampton, who require their hearing and balance in order to function in their work and social lives. I have already had part one and part two of the Pfizer vaccination. I have not, nor will I, visit any COVID hotspots during my time working in rural NSW, or during my travel to Queensland to take up my new employment. I take my work responsibilities seriously, and do not believe that I am a transmission risk to the people of Queensland, whom I intend to serve during this difficult period.

I must also remain fully employed during my time in Australia; so that the conditions of my TSS 482 VISA are not broken, forcing me to leave the country. Please would you permit me to enter Queensland; to take up my new residence and to

begin my new employment without quarantine delay?
Thank you for considering my application.

I was laying it on thick as you can see. Nevertheless, nothing happened. So, on the 30th of July, I called the QLD government to follow up on my application. Most of the time the phone rang for over an hour and nobody answered. On the one occasion I did manage to get through, on a Sunday afternoon of all occasions, I was told to add a follow up message to bolster my application on the health directions portal. So that is what I did:

Dear Dr Jeannette Young (QLD Chief Health Officer)
I called the Queensland government on 13 42 68 to check the progress of my application earlier this afternoon, and I was advised to send a follow up message to bolster my application. The rental lease at my current property comes to an end on the 2nd of August. I was only due to be on the road until I got to Brisbane for my induction on the 5th of August, and then begin my new job in Rockhampton on the 16th. My new rental property lease begins officially on the 11th of August in Rockhampton. Because I will now be essentially homeless from the 2nd of August, during the time that I am stuck in NSW, I would appreciate alacrity in the processing of my exemption if possible. Should you require a business contact to confirm the essential nature of my employment as an Audiologist in Rockhampton, I can provide references for you.
Regards
Tom

And still... nothing happened. Furthermore, by this point in time Delta had grown larger than Sydney and was beginning to infect its way south in greater numbers. Come the 2nd of August, cases of COVID 19 had already been recorded as far south as Wollongong. It wouldn't be long before it hit Vincentia and Sanctuary Point as well so once again, it was time to go. The million-dollar question was: go where?

Side note: I would like to give a special shout out to the British High Commission, in Australia, at this point in the tale. When I phoned them to seek assistance with the predicament that I was facing, I was met with an automated message telling me that all of their staff were currently very busy dealing with the pressures of COVID 19 back in the UK, and were therefore unavailable to take my call. For more information I should refer to their website. Suffice to say the phrase 'as useful as a chocolate teapot' springs to mind.

XV

PERIPATETIC

My time in Sanctuary Point ended with Tracy and Marty on the day my rental lease was terminated. After I had said my final goodbye to Victoria, I stayed with them on my final night. I was sensitive not to impose myself on them any longer than this. Marty had dual custody of his two kids, who came down from Sydney to live with him one week on and one week off, and I didn't want to be the person responsible for breaking the harmony of their family time. We hugged, wished each other good luck, and then they waved me off. The last I saw of them was in the Magna's rear-view mirror, as I drove to the end of the road to begin my nomadic life. At this point there were some things I did know, and there were some things that I didn't know.

I couldn't go North East because Delta was already rampant in this part of NSW. I also knew that I shouldn't go too far south, because I would eventually hit the Victorian border. Victoria was in lockdown, and even if I got in by some miracle, there was no guarantee that I would get out again. South Australia was the same, so I couldn't go too far west. I also couldn't go too far north either because even if I drove to the QLD border, along one of the lesser travelled inland routes such as the Mitchell Highway for instance, what would have happened when I got there? I didn't have my exemption yet, and Rockhampton had told me that they wanted to avoid paying the cost of a quarantine for me if possible. They were still betting on the QLD border restrictions being temporary at that point in time. So, in my mind I was left with the option of travelling to rural localities which currently had no confirmed cases of COVID. I could travel around in circles until the border restrictions were removed, or until I heard news about my exemption from the QLD government. With that rudimentary plan in mind I headed south, to Bega, the home of cheese.

I didn't know what I would do when I got to Bega. I initially thought about booking into a campsite and sleeping in the car. However, I arrived to discover that all the campsites had closed due to COVID, which threw that plan out of the window. Fortunately for me, I eventually stumbled across a very cheap motel with plenty of vacancies, who asked no questions, and were only too happy for my custom. It turned out that COVID 19 had hit the motel industry very hard across NSW, because nobody was travelling through anymore. This was great for me because it meant that I could turn up anywhere short notice and be guaranteed a bed for the night. But it was bad in the sense that all of the tourist attractions had also closed. COVID had turned rural Australia into a ghost town and it was a surreal time to see it. Bega for instance is famous for its cheese factory tour, but this had closed. So, I was only able to take pictures of it from the outside before being moved on by a man in a gas mask.

I tell people that I saw Australia during my time on the road, but really what I saw was an abandoned version of what Australia used to be. I headed west to Cooma, famous for its Snowy Hydro Discovery Centre. The tours had been discontinued because of COVID but I was given a free information pack by the skeleton crew manning the information desk. On to Adaminaby to see the Big Trout statue. COVID couldn't stop interested parties from being able to see the Trout fortunately, which was situated in a public park, but all the local wooden shops emulating the American west were unmistakably closed. I then travelled across the Great Dividing Range through the snow-covered mountains of the Kosciuszko National Park, 1480m to the top of Sawyers Hill, where I passed the wreck of an eighteen-wheeler truck; which had crashed through the mountain road barrier days earlier and was now hanging over a precipitous drop. No doubt the magnitude of the impending operation to retrieve a truck of that size in such an isolated spot, was not at the top of the local council's priority list all else considered. Beyond Sawyers Hill lay the Yarrangobilly Limestone Caves. I could see no signs of life inside the information centre when I arrived there, but I was surprised to see a car park partially filled with Asian tourists. I wasn't the only traveller making the most of a bad situation it seemed. The bumpy unsurfaced road out to the caves ended up costing me several of my glasses, which smashed within the plastic box that contained them. I encountered more signs of life in the town of Tumut, where I was relieved to find that the public toilets had not been closed, and then it was on to Wagga Wagga.

Wagga felt busy compared to the isolation that had courted me on the Snowy Mountains Highway, and even though several attractions were closed I was still able to take advantage of their wealth of: art galleries, memorial statues and botanical gardens. By this point in the journey I had become quite comfortable turning up at motels late in the evening, with confidence that the rooms were plentiful. Nonetheless, I was now beginning to get more questions from the staff manning reception. Where have you been? Why are you here? Which company do you work for? Australia was fast becoming a place where you needed to justify being wherever you happened to be. What also struck me as I explored was that the people of Wagga were wearing masks when they were walking around outside on the streets, and not just when they were inside shops or restaurants. I quickly learned to do the same. I was in Wagga for a couple of days and decided to try and call the QLD government again to follow up on my border restriction exemption application. I stayed on hold for one hour and forty-five mins, and gave it up as a bad job.

Tracy and Marty kept tabs on me during my travels, and when they heard that I had made it to Wagga Wagga they recommended that I should go and see Greggo. Greggo lived in the small town of Culcairn, not too far south of Wagga, on the way to the border town of Albury. Seeing as I had planned to go to Albury before heading west to Broken Hill, and I had time on my hands, I thought I might as well visit Greggo on the way. Greggo was an old friend of Tracy's; he had been the man that she hosted a radio show with all those years ago back in Blacktown. Tracy phoned ahead to tell him that I was coming and after I got a COVID test at a drive-in centre in Wagga, which came back negative, I subsequently drove down to meet him. Greggo was waiting for me at the end of his drive when I pulled up to his small farmhouse. He was a short portly gentleman with a kind face, and a woolly hat. *"We'll take your car if you don't mind"* he said *"my car's out of action at the moment"*. There was only one problem with this, my car was rammed with everything I owned and Greggo was not built for squeezing.

There was only one thing for it. We set about moving everything out of the front foot well and started stacking it behind the passenger seat, as tall as we could make it, whilst trying not to obscure my view out of the back window. After some grunting and groaning Greggo managed to jam himself into the passenger seat, and off we went. I didn't know this at the time but Greggo had planned a morning of activities for us, in the nearby town of

Holbrook, and I was blindly following his lead. As we drove along he regaled me with stories of how he had filled the airwaves with Tracy. Greggo used to do funny voices, and one of his radio characters was an old Scottish lady similar to the one played by Robin Williams in Mrs Doubtfire. We drove for a while until we reached a farm where another man, dressed in a baseball cap and gum boots, was waiting for us. I got the impression that Greggo was also meeting him for the first time. We both shook his hand and he invited us into his truck. I still wasn't exactly sure what was about to happen, but as he drove us out across the farm it became clear that this was a tour. I also learned that this farmer was planning on making tours part of his business, and we were there for him to practice on. Furthermore, Greggo was thinking about acquiring some chickens one day, and was keen to learn more about the process of keeping them.

We bounced along an uneven dirt track until we came to what can only be described as a sea of chickens, which parted to permit us to drive amongst them. The chickens were shepherded by two large Pyrenean Mountain Dogs. *"Aw, that one's got something caught around its neck"* Greggo said as we drove closer. It was true, one of the dogs had three pipes bolted around its neck in a triangular formation. *"Nah",* said the farmer, *"that one likes to jump through fences".* Once the tour was over, and I had asked as many questions about chicken feed that I could think of, we thanked the farmer for his time and we then headed into the centre of Holbrook; for a sausage roll and a cup of tea. Sitting at a table, processing exactly what I had just been a part of, Greggo began to tell me more about himself. Just like every other native Aussie I had encountered on my travels, he didn't disappoint.

He had originally met Tracy in a club called Bobby McGee.

He had played the piano and the drums since the age of eleven, inspired after hearing the music of Elton John who had been his hero ever since. He originally trained as an electrician for four years, before moving into the business of air conditioning maintenance and repair. He took care to tell me that funnily enough, there were actually lots of black people in Blacktown, and was interested to know whether there were any black people in my native city of Bristol. Greggo also told me that he had never seen a person of colour, growing up in Australia, until he came to the UK. Continuing with the theme of spot the black person, Greggo's travels had taken him to New York where he had allegedly paid a bouncer $20 dollars to get into a night club, after he was previously denied entry, where it just so happened that Michael Jordan and Shaq were having a private party. He was the only white guy in the building and after some Dutch courage he asked MJ for an autograph and he said: *"I don't do that when I'm out man sorry."* He didn't approach Shaq apparently, because he was too scary.

Times were different back then. During Greggo's time in the US, he found himself in a restaurant where he was approached by a five-year-old girl who engaged him in an innocent conversation. He then got talking to the little girl's father, who was sat at the table across. The little girl's father eventually invited Greggo to accompany them, so that they could show him around New York, and as they were walking down the street they caught a glimpse of some very attractive women conversing outside a shop. At which point, the Dad said to Greggo that he could borrow his daughter if he wanted; so that he could approach these women and while they were distracted by her cuteness, he would have a chance to speak to them and pick one of them up. Greggo said that he didn't take the Dad up on his offer because they were an African American family, and it would therefore have been difficult to pass off the man's daughter as his own. If I took a moment, I could probably think of a few more reasons why it was wise for Greggo to decline this offer.

Greggo had spent a large portion of his thirteen weeks long service leave travelling around Europe, which is how he came to visit the UK in the mid-90's. During his time in London he was lucky enough to get a ticket for a charity AIDS gig, which he had seen advertised in Vanity Fair. The headliner for this gig was no other than Greggo's hero Elton John. Elton mingled with the crowd after he had performed, and Greggo managed to shake his hand, but he was too star struck to say anything much to his chagrin. He did, however, manage to get a selfie with Dannii Minogue, after managing to catch her eye and engage her in a chant of: *"Aussie Aussie Aussie, Oi Oi Oi"*. After we had enjoyed our tea and sausage roll, Greggo asked me whether I could take him to the supermarket, so that he could do some shopping. I was happy to oblige seeing as he had treated me to lunch. My tea had gone straight through me, so after I had dropped Greggo off at the shops I asked one of the staff where the public toilets were. I was told to: *"turn right at the submarine"*. Thinking that the submarine must have been a pub, I stared around like a lost child as I looked for a building that met the description. In response to my confusion, the lady I had asked for directions gesticulated again and went: *"you know.... the submarine"*. As I looked harder I then felt like a fool when an enormous black submarine came into focus, planted in the middle of the park over the road. Turns out the submarine is what Holbrook is famous for.

I said farewell to Greggo after we had shared a meal in a Chinese restaurant that was so well hidden, I felt like we were the only ones who must have known about it. We ate our food amongst a completely empty sea of tables. I felt that this is what it must be like when millionaires go out for Chinese, and reserve an entire restaurant. After I had dropped Greggo back home, and re-organised the Magna, we shook hands and he wished me all the best with the QLD government. It's funny that Greggo chose that moment to say that, because right then the QLD Government showed up.

XVI

IT WASN'T ME SIR, HONEST

I received a phone call from an unknown number about fifteen minutes after I had left Greggo's house. It was a call from a delegate of the QLD Government's Health Directions Exemption Service, called Jo, who wished to follow up my exemption request. She didn't pull her punches. I was told that there was currently no appetite for anybody driving into QLD for the foreseeable future; so new residents **must enter QLD by air and complete fourteen days mandatory quarantine, in government arranged accommodation,** at their own expense. Exemptions from these requirements will only be granted in **extremely exceptional circumstances,** by the Chief Health Officer. My circumstances were not exceptional enough. Jo crushed any lingering hope I had by concluding that even if she put my application through to the Chief Health Officer, it would certainly be denied based on past experience.

While Jo recognised that I wanted to enter QLD with my car, because this was my home currently and contained all of my possessions, I was nonetheless still required to fly into Brisbane and serve my hotel quarantine. I would just have to suck it up and make alternative arrangements for my freight. When I asked whether the fact that I am double vaccinated held any sway, she told me that even vaccinated people can potentially carry the

Delta variant, so the government are not willing to take that risk. I detected a trace of sympathy in her voice by the end of the call, and she finished by telling me that my pending quarantine exemption request wouldn't be progressed for consideration, by the Chief Health Officer, until I gave the go ahead. If Jo didn't receive a response from me within seven days, then she would assume that I no longer wished to proceed. We said our goodbyes and I sank back into my seat as the true gravity of what she had said washed over me.

I didn't have any solutions for the problems that Jo had presented me with in that moment, the only thing I did have immediate control over was where I went next. So, I kept breathing and went to Albury to see what the tide would bring. True to form I checked into a motel later than evening and the owner was only too happy to see me; I was the only customer who had graced his premises all day. There didn't seem to be any point in heading out to Broken Hill anymore, because it looked like all hope of killing time long enough for the QLD government to remove their border restrictions with NSW was lost. Furthermore, if I wanted to avoid the financial cost of a Brisbane quarantine, as my new boss desired, I needed to enter QLD from a place that was not considered a hotspot. At present, all of NSW was considered a hotspot and so was Victoria (VIC) and South Australia (SA). I was all out of states, or so I thought.

That is when I had a fine idea because up until Albury, I had been forgetting one state that had miraculously managed to elude COVID 19 for the past twelve months. The Australian Capital Territory (ACT) had had fewer cases in the past year than any other state or territory, even after accounting for its smaller population size. Canberra had confounded epidemiologists because at no point had they banned NSW residents from visiting. This revelation was a lightbulb moment for me because the ACT was still in the green, as far as QLD were concerned, which meant that people from Canberra could travel to Brisbane without having to quarantine, as long as they could prove that they hadn't been in a hotspot within the past fourteen days. I had taken care to avoid the ACT, when I first left Sanctuary Point, because the ACT government had published a list of NSW Local Government Areas (LGA's) who were on their no entry list; due to those areas contracting local cases of the virus. Jervis Bay and the surrounding region was a banned LGA. But I wasn't in Jervis Bay anymore, I was in Albury. Not only was I in Albury, but I had tested negative for COVID not more than twenty-four hours earlier. Furthermore, Albury was not on the ACT's list of LGA's banned from entry. So, I hatched a cunning plan.

If I could get into the ACT and book myself a hotel for fourteen days, which after some calculations I could see would be much cheaper than the advertised price of a Brisbane quarantine, this would mean that I would have satisfied the QLD government's requirements. I would have to find a way of sending my car to Rockhampton somehow, so that my possessions would be waiting for me when I arrived, but I figured that I would worry about that during my two weeks in the ACT. I thought it was a stroke of genius, and what I was doing seemed to make sense to people because when I called my new CEO in Brisbane to explain myself, she supported me one hundred per cent and even offered to pay for the costs as part of my relocation package. So, I packed up that very evening, and headed for the capital.

The final leg of this journey, along the Barton Highway, was a nerve-wracking drive because even though I felt what I was doing was technically legal on paper, I had read about the dreaded ACT border checkpoints. These had been imposed on traffic the past few weeks to carry out the LGA restrictions that the ACT had imposed on NSW, especially on the highways linking Greater Sydney. I arrived in Canberra on the 6th of August after dark, and mercifully avoided any checkpoints. I could only imagine trying to explain the quite frankly unbelievable circumstances surrounding my arrival to a checkpoint police officer; who I suspect would have directed me towards a mandatory government quarantine, just because it would take less effort than listening to me tell a tall tale on the side of the road.

I pulled into a cheap motel in Lyneham, where the young woman at the check in desk asked me where I had come from. *"Albury"* I said. She paused for a second, and looked through a laminated list of LGA's that she had printed out on the desk. *"What was that name again?"* she said *"Albury"* I repeated unblinkingly. *"Hmmm, is that one of the problem areas?"* she enquired to which I replied *"no"* quite earnestly. *"Okay, well it will be $99 for the night, you can park anywhere"*. One thing that gave me away as an outsider to the ACT that night, which I didn't fully grasp until the following day, was that I had instinctively put on a mask before I entered the motel reception. Masks had never been mandatory in the ACT, and I didn't see many people wearing them the following morning.

Before I went to bed I searched the internet to book a two week stay in a hotel closer to the centre of Canberra. If I was going to stay in Australia's capital for two weeks I thought, I wanted to make the most of it by being close to the tourist attractions. This was another rookie error and in hindsight I should have booked a week in two separate hotels. Not five minutes after I had booked my two week stay at the Mercure, who had the best deal, I received a phone call from the hotel to ask why I was booking a fourteen day stay. Fourteen days reeked of self-quarantine, and I realised my mistake the moment she asked me the question. I explained to her that I needed to stay at the hotel because I was in the process of transitioning between residences; my current rental lease had come to an end, but COVID had stopped me from entering my new residence. So, I needed a buffer while this was all being sorted. This was technically the truth, and I tend to find that the best lies are in fact subtly tailored versions of the truth. She said this was OK, but if I have been near a COVID 19 hotspot then I must contact the ACT government immediately. I reassured her that I was actually in Lyneham at the present time. I then went on the offensive: *"Oh by the way will there be parking available when I arrive in the morning?"* looking to deflect *"Oh yes Sir there is parking available at the front and the rear of the hotel, but you will need to check in before you can gain access to the rear car park. Was there anything else I can help you with?"* she said. *"No that's great thank you, I will see you tomorrow"* I ended the call while I was back in the driving seat.

That felt like a close shave. I couldn't shake the feeling that even though I was going out of my way to follow the rules, I still came across to others like a man on the run. Generalising the truth to avoid suspicion, because the truth itself was completely unbelievable. There was a moment during my time in Canberra where I was accidentally locked inside a KFC toilet, because the door had a faulty mechanism. In the heat of the moment, as I pulled on the door handle in vein, I genuinely thought for a moment that the ACT government had set a sting to catch me.

After bouncing off the walls for a while, I eventually thought to pull the emergency cord and one of the staff came to release me apologetically. It's strange what stress does to your imagination. When I checked into the Mercure the following afternoon, the man at the reception desk asked me the same questions that his colleague had done on the phone the night before. I was ready for it this time, and gave him a much smoother rendition of the same answer I had given to his colleague. *"Ah he said, a few of our guests have had the same thing happen to them, its crazy stuff all this COVID business hey"*. *"You have no idea"* I thought to myself, as he handed me my room key with a smile.

My first week in Canberra was great. I went out every day to see as many of the sights as I could, which were plentiful. Being a native to Canberra herself, Tash was able to give me some tips on the best places to visit. Some things were closed because of COVID but most things were open. Once again it felt like I had taken a time machine back before COVID. I even managed to locate a Canberra based car transport express company to deliver the Magna to Rockhampton. The only pain was that even though they were happy to transport cars containing people's possessions, said possessions had to all fit in the boot and could not be loose on the back seats or in the foot wells. This is apparently to avoid restricting the transport staff's ability to fully adjust the seating positions, and to prevent their view out the windows from being obstructed.

The Magna was busting at the seams so I had some sacrificing to do. Late one cold Canberra evening; overseen by a guest enjoying a cigarette on her balcony who had nothing better to do but watch me work, under the illumination of the street lamp overhanging the rear Mercure car park, I went about taking all of my worldly possessions out of the Magna. I laid them out in the car park, flea market style, and systematically threw everything that I could afford to lose in a skip across the road. It was a bit of a wrench chucking away all of those items after they had come so far (1112 km to be precise), I was hoping that bringing them along would have saved me some money when I eventually arrived in Rockhampton, but I didn't have much choice in the matter. It took a few hours to do, but eventually the job was done and I said goodbye to the Magna mid-way through my first week, fingers crossed I would see it again once I got to QLD. Canberra had such good public transport that I didn't need a car during my time there.

I love it when a plan comes together, and as I neared the end of my first week everything seemed to be looking up. I was so confident at this stage that when I received a second call from Jo, at 8:30am that same week, asking whether I would like to proceed with my quarantine exemption application, I said *"no thank you leave it with me"*. It seemed incredibly unlikely that I would get one, and it looked like I wouldn't be needing one anymore anyway. Unfortunately, there was another man who had also decided to come to Canberra that week, who was about to blow my genius plan clean out of the water. On the 15th of August at 5pm, news broke around the world that the ACT were going into a snap seven-day lockdown, after over a year of remaining essentially COVID free. In a freak act of mistaken identity caused by a freak coincidence, when the news broke that the Delta strain had been introduced to Canberra by a man in his twenties, my family and friends thought that man might have been me. I subsequently received lots of messages that night that went like this:

"The plot of this film really is getting ridiculous now. I'm

genuinely starting to believe that you maybe cursed. Did you anger a gypsy at any point?"

"I heard the news that I didn't want to hear on the BBC this morning that there is a case of COVID in Canberra, I just hope this doesn't mess things up for you"

"Just reading that the ACT is going into lockdown. Does that bugger up any of your travel plans?"

"Australian capital goes into snap lockdown. Have you got a new plan then? This is all sounding more stressful than originally anticipated."

"They bringing in the military?"

"ACT in lockdown! (Face palm emoji)"

"Tom, I gather from the news that Canberra will be going into a one-week lockdown, how or will this be affecting you? I'm assuming that you are still COVID free? I thought you were nearly there"

"That wasn't you causing the lockdown in Canberra?"

The best made plans of mice and men often go awry. The mystery man in his twenties who was actually responsible remains somewhat controversial. According to the exposure sites released by the ACT government at the time, patient zero was at a city nightclub until 4.45am on Sunday morning, but still managed to attend church service at 10.30am the same day. Then he went off to do some shopping before ending the day with an evening drinking session in a city bar. Australians were torn as to how to receive this information, was patient zero a villain or some kind of legend with a go-hard, go-long attitude. The ACT's Chief Minister, Andrew Barr, stated at the time that who the man was and how he contracted COVID was *"entirely unimportant at the moment because it will do absolutely nothing to address the*

112

situation that we face today". He was right, knowing who it was wasn't going to help me either. I still needed to get to QLD and staying in Canberra any longer made no logical sense, where once it did, as the ACT itself was now a hotspot.

I called Brisbane to tell them what had happened but they already knew. I explained that I can either stay in the ACT and hope that the snap lockdown only lasts for seven days as advertised, which I doubted it would (and I was correct), or I could fly to Brisbane on the nearest flight and get the quarantine over and done with. They agreed to fund the latter, resigned to the fact that all other options had now been fully exhausted.

XVII

DÉJÀ VU

Aspiring residents looking to relocate to the Sunshine State needed to obtain an entry pass before they crossed the border. The type of entry pass that they were eligible for depended on: their current circumstances, where they were coming from, and what they intended to do once they entered QLD. The border restriction entry passes were coded alphabetically, which made it easier for police to process people when they arrived. After completing the online application form, I was granted a Q Pass. To clarify, people in Q class could only enter QLD by air and had to do fourteen days mandatory quarantine upon arrival in a government hotel. NSW/QLD border zone residents who were undertaking border zone travel for an essential purpose were X class. Freight and logistics operators were F class. Specialist or essential workers critical to the QLD supply chain were S class. Then there was Z class. If the entry passes were the Mighty Morphin Power Rangers then Z Class was definitely the White Ranger. I saw one of the pilots sporting a Z class QR code when I arrived in Brisbane. Z pass holders were workers who were granted an exemption direct from the Chief Health Officer, and could subsequently cross the border as often as necessary to perform their function.

Canberra airport was essentially deserted when I arrived for departure, and there were only eight people on the flight to

Brisbane, six in economy and two in business class. This makes sense because what sane person would be travelling to Brisbane under the current circumstances, if they didn't have to. When I arrived at the airport, all of the passengers from each flight were separated into police processing pens. Four flights were ahead of us in a queue of pens which were formed longitudinally, by retractable belt barriers, along the right-hand side of an endless terminal walkway. The left side of the terminal walkway was empty so that: federal police, cleaners, and other airport staff, could walk up and down the pens to interact with the passengers and flight crew. One freckled young woman, whom I was sharing a pen with, was stood behind me as we waited for the police to reach us. She was on the phone to somebody and sounded very distressed. She was talking in a very strained manner and started cursing in ever more high-pitched tones.

From what I could overhear she was worried about whether she had applied for the correct QLD entry pass. She had applied for an X class, and was now second guessing herself. I had a suspicion that her stress had ignited after witnessing what both of us had just witnessed. One of the airport managers who had apparently been tasked with assisting police with organising the people in each pen, suddenly lost his cool: *"I HAVE HAD IT WITH AIR CREW TRYING TO TELL ME HOW TO DO MY JOB, WE HAVE HAD HUNDREDS OF PEOPLE THROUGH HERE WE KNOW WHAT NEEDS TO BE DONE. I'VE HAD TO LISTEN TO IT ALL DAY AND I WILL NOT TOLERATE IT"*. His voice rang out through the terminal and brought everything to an awkward standstill. The processing teams and the flight crews were at odds with each other; because the pilots and their attendants were typically used to flashing their badges and walking right on through any barrier that the passengers had to honour. They were looking to get through the airport ASAP so that they could get to the next flight that they were due to man. Now though, they had to be processed like everybody else.

"I don't want to be shouted at by a fucking police officer at the checkpoint for having the wrong pass" said the freckled woman: *"Fuck, what should I fucking do? Look they're walking up and down now. Why won't they speak to me?"* When the police finally came to speak to her, it turned out that her worse fears were true. She was informed that she would have to reapply for a standard Q entry pass, because even though her last permanent address had resided on the border between NSW and QLD, she had still spent time in Canberra before flying into Brisbane. Canberra was now classified as a hotspot. This meant quarantining in a hotel like everybody else and not at a residence of her choosing. This news turned out to be all too much for her, and she had an emotional breakdown. She began to: cry, convulse, and moan all at once, and soon had to be cordoned off to the side and consoled by a spare officer.

I was processed by a personable and dry witted police officer called Lynne. *"1992"* she had queried when looking at my date of birth *"I'd have thought you were older than that, but you are wearing a hat I suppose"*. She explained that they were running out of rooms in Brisbane, so there was a question mark about potentially sending some people out to the Gold Coast instead. *"Rockhampton, you poor thing. I'm a Yeppoon girl myself, hated Rockhampton. You'll see, lookup Yeppoon in the hotel, and get local friends to send you food once you know your room number"*. Lynne proceeded to register me while I was in the holding pen, she asked to see my tenancy agreement and

116

employment contract before scanning the QR code on my entry pass. *"How much luggage have you got? Four pieces, Christ! I don't carry that much and I'm a girl"* said Lynne after she had finished registering me on her iPad. Eight people from my flight went into the pen and only five came out. The freckled lady was taken to hospital, and the other two were transiting so they got processed quickly and moved on. The remaining five of us were escorted through the airport to the exit where two minibuses were due to take us to the hotel. Another police officer was manning the pick-up zone and before the minibuses arrived she turned to us all and said, with a puzzled look: *"You're from Canberra right. You guys knew that you would have to quarantine when you came here right?"* It was said with the rhetorical inference of: if you knew, why bother?

There were no military personnel to help me with my luggage this time, in fact everybody around me was very hands off due to concerns about the Delta strain. When we arrived at the hotel we had to change our masks and gel our hands before entering the lobby, as directed by a nurse. Once we were inside, it was déjà vu as the sergeant of the Brisbane police force gave us our COVID Miranda warning. Fines for leaving our rooms were now as high as $13,000. Police took our details and checked us in before I was eventually taken to my cell. *"Do me a favour mate, kick that rubber shoe over to me when you have your luggage sorted. See ya"*.

The door clicked shut undeniably, silence ensued and my second quarantine began. Swab tests were performed on Day one and Day two, I also received phone calls from the QLD Government on Day two to check whether I had any new symptoms. I thought I was ready for my swab tests, and assumed the position I had learned in Sydney, but this time I was directed to keep my head

117

neutral and stay orthogonal to the open door. There was another swab on Day five, and around this time I also received welcome confirmation that the Magna had arrived safely in Rockhampton. Lorraine, a lady who sounded like she had smoked a thousand cigarettes, and gargled with gravel, from Capricorn Towing did me the honour.

Half way through the quarantine the QLD government informed me that due to recent changes to their Border Restrictions Direction, my right of entry to Brisbane had been suspended until the 8th of September. This meant that if I was not already in QLD, then I was now not permitted to enter even if I had a pass. Had I not got out of Canberra when I did, I would have had to have stayed there and reapplied for another entry pass after the 8th. That was lucky, because QLD's hotel quarantine system must have been nearing full capacity when I arrived; the system was now housing more than five thousand people. On Day eleven, the QLD government called me again to check my health and on Day twelve my final COVID swab test came back negative. On Day thirteen I received a phone call from QLD health to advise me to call reception and arrange a check out slot, which would be done under police escort. I dutifully called reception and booked the 9:30am slot. Due to a glitch in the matrix, half an hour later I then received a call from hotel reception asking me when I would like to check out on day fourteen. I am not sure what happened there but I was surprised to find that the 9:30am slot was available when I re-booked my exit.

On the final day I was escorted to the hotel lobby by a balding policeman keen to keep things moving. After check out I was escorted to the glass door, where I was shown the street. My second quarantine was over, and I was free… again.

XVIII

NOT SOMEBODY TO MESS WITH

Before I flew to Rockhampton, I had to complete basic training at headquarters in Brisbane. This is where I met the CEO. She was the person who had interviewed me for the job in Rocky, over the phone back in Sanctuary Point, and this was the first time I was seeing her in person. She was a native Queenslander from the rural town of Jundah. A self-confessed local girl made good, with an interesting past. She was fascinated by history and Ancient Egypt, and was not averse to travelling out to isolated and dangerous locations in North Africa, with nothing more than hand luggage, in order to satisfy her craving for knowledge and adventure. In fact, one dream she still held was to one day walk across the dividing line of what used to be Mesopotamia, although she admitted that due to the current political climate this was unlikely to occur in her lifetime. I had originally been captured by her philosophy that it was actually a selfish act on her part to offer her staff continuous training and progression, in addition to a competitive salary, because she wanted her staff to stay with the company for as long as possible. *"I don't want you to leave the company and move on"* she had said to me over the phone, and even though I have learned to take any verbal promise made within the world of business with a heavy pinch of salt, even I had to admit that was a great pitch.

As a child she had excelled in track and field events at

school, and following this trend she went on to train and qualify as a PE teacher. Her first job was working in a rough area of Brisbane, which is where she got the chance to prove what an immovable object she could be. The headmaster came to her not long after she started her new position and told her that: *"you must control these children on Thursday afternoons, because if you don't they'll jump the fence"*. What he meant by this was that because the kids had PE on Thursday afternoon, outdoors in the playing field, the hardnuts would elect to jump over the perimeter fence because that was pension day. They would be aiming to go out and snatch the pensions (all paid in cash back then), out of the elderly people's handbags and wallets.

One day, one of the twelve-year-old boys that she was teaching that afternoon jumped the fence. When this boy refused to come back at once, the CEO had hopped the fence herself and caught him in the same way that a stoat catches a rabbit. She wore him down through pure exhaustion. 5km later, the pursuit was over and he was done. She began to drag him back to school by his wrist. The boy had one last trick up his sleeve, he decided to sink his teeth into the CEO's wrist (she still has the scar) in one last ditch attempt to escape. She responded in kind by stepping on his toes until he released her. It took two hours to drag him back to the school, where class was well and truly over. However, not to be denied, our heroine made this boy sit through the next class that she was due to teach, to drive the point home that nobody misses her lessons. She bumped into this boy eleven years later where he was working in the local chip shop, and lo and behold he recognised her and thanked her for what she had done with a free meal. He was now married with children of his own, and thought that her tenacity had been the making of him.

After many years of running outback rehabilitation

programs for troubled children, single handed, she eventually went on to retrain as an Audiologist, and soon became Head of Department in Brisbane before moving on to become the CEO. She showed me around during my induction and introduced me to all of the movers and shakers, including my new state manager. As per usual there was some more paperwork to sign. Everybody seemed mostly interested in hearing about whether quarantine was as bad as everyone thought it was. My induction in Brisbane took two days, and I was then due to fly out to Rockhampton to finally meet the people I would be working with directly. So, at 8:45am on the 1st of September, after a month of living the peripatetic lifestyle, I finally caught a one-way flight out to the City of the Three S's on the Tropic of Capricorn.

XIX

I'VE GOT A LETTER FOR YOU

Sin, sweat, and sorrow. That's what early migrants bound for Rockhampton came to know it for supposedly. I can tell you that Rockhampton is without doubt a city steeped in history and tradition, but it's also a city of contrast. The abstract exhibits of the Rockhampton Art Gallery, the progressive music of the Riverside Festival, and the highfalutin ideas of the CQ University, juxtapose the conservative lifeblood of the railway and coalmines which carve a very literal path right through the central business district. After I had exited Rockhampton Airport, my first job was to pick up the Magna, so I took an Uber to Capricorn Towing, which is where it was meant to be waiting for me. Lorraine was there to greet me with her unmissable Tom Wait's voice. There it was, sat in the middle of the lot. I took the keys and unlocked the doors to find that my glass thermometer had exploded mercury all over the parcel shelf. Suffice to say it was very hot in that car when I opened the door, after it had been baking in the QLD sun for the past few days. I signed some release paperwork, loaded up, and headed into town to find the estate agents.

Just like the big wigs in Brisbane had been, the property manager at McGrath was also keen to hear what the Brisbane quarantine had been like, and asked me lots of questions about it before she went on to explain all the rules of my new apartment. I felt a bit like a soldier returning from the war; which surprised me because quarantine really wasn't anything like being in Vietnam, based on the harrowing documentary footage I have seen. People's interest in it showed me just how daunting a prospect being locked in a room for two weeks is for many. For me, it was almost effortless; just a natural extension of my introverted personality. But people's haunted reactions to my descriptions of what it had been like day to day, helped me to understand the immense trouble that the various state governments had had with people trying to escape their quarantine hotels. Just like polar bears at the zoo, most human beings are not well designed for being locked alone with their thoughts for extended periods. In other words, the thing that a significant number of people would be tortured with most effectively, as described in George Orwell's Room 101, is the empty room itself.

Side Note: *Some of you might be wondering how I managed to secure a new rental apartment in Rockhampton, while I was living eighteen hours away dealing with the proverbial chaos in NSW and the ACT. Well, I had a secret weapon called Sommer. Sommer was part of my new team in Rockhampton and a local tour de force. If being an Audiologist makes me a pilot, Sommer is air traffic control and we would most likely crash into each other and burn without her. Well, I would anyway. When I emailed Rockhampton to introduce myself, Sommer selflessly took it upon herself to find me an apartment. She found an apartment, viewed it in her lunchbreak, and filed a commercial application on my behalf. All I had to do was sign the paperwork and make sure that the rent was paid while I was trying to get into QLD. The company ended up covering the costs for me as part of my relocation package. I couldn't have asked for more. How did I know whether it would be any good? I hear you ask. I don't wish to rile up the feminists here, but when Sommer told me*

123

that she had showed the apartment to all the ladies in the office, and they were all in agreement that they would be happy to live there, I was never in doubt.

I was given four keys, two large and two small. The larger keys opened the front doors, one of the small keys opened the post box, and the other small key… I still don't know what that one does. When I first arrived at the property I realised what Sommer had meant when she said it was secure. I was meant to live in Unit two. There were four white doors in front of me, and none of them had any numbers on them. In fact, the doors had no identifying features of any kind. I stood there scratching my head for a while, thinking about how I should tackle this problem, when one of the doors opened and a short hirsute man appeared wearing a light blue t-shirt and thongs. Squinting in to the sun he jutted his chin in my direction. I introduced myself and explained that I was a new tenant and was trying to find my way into Unit two. It turned out that the man was called Bevan and he was to be my new neighbour. Bevan showed me which door was mine and we exchanged pleasantries for a little while. Bevan informed me that he wasn't employed right now but he usually drives trucks and performs deliveries.

Bevan was quite keen to show me my post-box, and once I opened it I understood why. At the front of the property was a large wooden block, with several stainless-steel mailboxes attached to it. *"Australia Post are always putting my mail in the wrong mailbox"* Bevan told me. *"The thing is, Centrelink don't have my address on their records, so I have had to use yours"*. When I turned my key and opened the Unit two mailbox, a mountain of letters came tumbling out of it. As I filed through them, I realised that some of them were for me, some of them were for Bevan, some of them were for his girlfriend, and several seemed to be for the previous tenants who had not cancelled their post. Weirdly, there was also an analogue passport sized photograph of a blonde lady striking a selfie pose. *"Friend of yours?"* I asked Bevan. *"Nah"* Bevan chuckled as he examined his letters. He seemed pleased as punch. Thinking about it, I suppose he had just won the lottery in a way because I was now his only neighbour; there wasn't anybody living in Unit one. So, when he had initially found out that Centrelink didn't have his address on record, I presume he had to take a guess as to which Unit would get a new tenant first. My presence confirmed that he must have gone for Unit two and won out. It did mean, however, that I was now sharing a mailbox with two other people, in the form of Bevan and his girlfriend.

I said my goodbye's to Bevan and began unpacking the Magna. It was while I was moving my stuff upstairs that I had my 'Back to the Future' moment. Not five minutes after I started moving in, I heard the humming of an engine through the open door leading to the car park. I went down there to investigate and came across a Postman dismounting from a small white scooter, heavily laden with large yellow saddle bags. He was wearing: a yellow helmet with a visor, tinted silver goggles, a high visibility polo shirt, black Velcro boots, brown trousers, a pair of fingerless gloves, and he had a package in his hands. *"Are you Thomas?"* he enquired. *"Yes"* I replied. *"Ah fantastic mate, you're a lifesaver"*. I was so stunned by the timing of this man's arrival that I rushed upstairs to grab my smartphone to capture the moment. *"Oh, I'm not sure about that"* he had said bashfully when I reappeared to snap a photograph of him. I signed for the parcel and away he went. It was a book that I had ordered weeks earlier, which had been redirected from my address in Sanctuary Point. Remarkable, I felt just like Marty McFly.

XX

SALT OF THE EARTH

To be honest my assimilation into Rockhampton, and ingratiating myself with my new team, was pretty eventless. Other than the usual challenges of learning the ropes in a new job role, I was happy. My new supervisor was highly experienced, good humoured and tolerant. My colleagues were accommodating and kind, and they had run a highly successful service together for several years before I showed up. All I really had to do was do as I was told, for the most part, and try not to screw things up. Straightforward really. I even had an eighteen-month career progression plan, and I now got monthly bonuses for my efforts. I was content. It had taken almost three years to get there but I was now pretty content. In fact, my immediate past experience had taught me how things could be much worse for sure. So, this chapter isn't about me, its dedicated to the people of Rockhampton and their eccentric nature. My appearance here didn't faze them one tiny bit:

GARY

Gary is licensed in second-hand goods, and I bought my first fridge from him not long after I arrived in Rocky. The thing is, I went out to buy a fridge and I came back with poetry. I found my way to a second-hand store where there was initially no sign of anybody. The lot surrounding the shop was an Aladdin's cave of everything you could think of: insect screens, rusty bed posts, window frames, tyres, ladders, mail boxes, step ladders, guttering, taps, sinks, lawnmowers, hose clamps, drawers, tables and bird cages. I navigated my way through the maze until I could see white tip-ex writing on the shop window, with Gary's name on it, so I entered the premises to see a wizened man tucked away in the back behind a stable door. He was sat in a deck chair reading a book. *"Gary?"* I said and the man stirred *"Hello, I'm Tom we spoke yesterday on Facebook marketplace". "Oh yeah what are you after"* Gary said with a grizzled voice. He rose from his chair and made his way towards me. His voice faded in and out as he meandered through the path that he had carved through the labyrinth of hoarded items. By modern standards the shop must have been a lawsuit waiting to happen. Stuff was sticking out from unbolted shelves, things were stacked loose on top of other things, and pointy objects were hanging from the ceiling.

Nevertheless, Gary appeared from a side passage and took some old curtains off of a set of fridges, in the middle of which was my Westinghouse. Gary had a moustache, sunlight faded tattoos all up his arms, and on each of his fingers. He wore a short sleeve checked shirt, and sported seasoned yellow lower incisors which showed their pulp as they balanced the smouldering cigarette in his mouth. He was seventy-four years old. *"Yeah good fridge that one mate, oh it's a good one, I got it from The Range that one I think. Right grab the end of it here, so that it doesn't fall over".* I helped Gary to duck walk the fridge over the lip of the front door to get it out into the yard. *"Right, let's see if it gets cold"* said Gary muttering to himself while he went away to fetch an extension cable. It was while Gary and I were stood there waiting for the fridge to get cold that the real fun began:

Gary: You've got to put yourself out there if you're fair dinkum mate. People work hard for their money so you've got to give them a good product you know what I mean? What do you do with yourself then?

Me: I'm an Audiologist

Gary: Audiologist, a.u.d.i.o.l.o.g.i.s.t (Gary spelled out the letters one by one). Audio that's ears right, and sound?

Me: Yeah, hearing aids and hearing loss that's right

Gary: You know what I am don't you? A philologist. You know what that is don't you? That's a person who knows all about words and definitions. I've been doing it for years now, I learn new words every day, and the thing is right, eventually you start using words that you would never normally think of. The worst thing you can call somebody is an idiot right, you know I hear blokes come up to me and say there is no such thing as the ice age, and I say to them mate before we go into this, your lack of knowledge prevents you from understanding any explanation that I would make about the proof of the ice age. We developed from hairy apes you see, people don't know. Six billion years ago it all happened right. There are too many people out there using words and have no idea what they mean. Never use a word that you can't spell, that's what I say. You've got to use your encephalon right, you know what that is? Another word for your brain see: encephalon, encephalogram, see how it all flows together. It's like a piece of steel, right. You look at a piece of steel and try to figure out how much it costs, and you know the price of the other bits of steel around it, then you can figure out how much that other piece is worth, you know what I mean? What word would you use for that then do you think?

Me: Extrapolate?

Gary: Yeah nah I wouldn't use that one but you might have it right there, how do you spell that one: e.x.t.r.a.p.o.l.a.t.e, right? Nah. I'm getting old you see so I can't do it as well as I used to, old grey matter is fading you know, but you have to train the brain you see, that's why they say that we only use ten per cent of it right. Expand, learn words every day and you won't be braindead. A lot of blokes are brain dead right, like a tree, just sucking in oxygen. Not worth talking to. Right, where are you parked? Green car over there is it?

Between us, and with help from a lady who was passing by, we got the fridge into the back of the Magna. Gary wanted cash, which I didn't carry. So, I gave him my driving license as collateral and went to the cash machine to get some. Upon my return, our conversation continued:

Gary: There are people out there with degrees who don't know anything right, teachers even don't know what they're talking about. I didn't go to school when I was young, I did about four years and that was it you know. I tell you I heard a teacher teaching a child about lactic acid, you know about lactic acid in the body right, and I told him I said you know you are teaching this all wrong. He said what do you mean? I said about lactic acid I don't know where you got that from but it's wrong. You're a teacher and you don't even know that, they don't like it though when you tell 'em, they won't admit it. Thick as shit they are. Tell you what, a lot of people right if they don't know a word they pretend like they do. You have got to be here in person if

129

you want to run a business mate, if you hire people and leave 'em, what they do is give stuff to their mates for free. Before you know it you're bankrupt. Hey come over here a second:

Gary led me over to another deck chair out in the yard where he makes himself comfortable, and lights another cigarette:

Gary: Loquacious and voluble, you know those ones. It's like poetry, here, you listen to this. I'm going to give you a memorandum:

Although we smiled and seemed to care
Tears do fall when no one is there
The loss is ours, the grief I hide
No one can see the ache inside
It's been a sad and lonely year
And loving thoughts bring many a tear
Now one year had passed
I truly know how much I miss you Rita
Sunshine passes, and shadows fall
And only the remnants remain
But I hope our love and memories
Will outlast them all

Gary: What bit did you like the best?

Me: I quite liked the line 'no one can see the ache inside'.

Gary: See how that word has to be there because it wouldn't work right. People come and ask me to put them together for valentine's days you see, I wrote that and I play a bit of guitar. *Have you ever noticed how when you don't say anything to people, they will tell you everything about them?*

130

SIDE NOTE: The immaculate irony of this revelation, was the most memorable part of the whole conversation for me I must admit. Alan Bennett could not have done better.

Gary: Here come through a minute. Gary proceeds to lead me through to the back of the shop, where there is a small cubbyhole, and sits down on another chair. I was content to lean against one of his other working fridges. He picked up an empty tin can with the label ripped off, and stubbed out his cigarette before continuing:

Gary: What do you think is going to happen in the future then?

Me: I think automation will be something to watch out for.

Gary: Automation, how do you spell that auto… what n or me, little m, then ation. Right, a.u.t.o.m.a.t.i.o.n that's a good one. That's robots isn't it, hey is that like when you call up a place and a voice goes press one for such and such press two for whatever. Yeah I was talking to a Sheila I know, and she thought I was crazy and I said nah they have got robots answering the phone here you know. Automation yeah, they have got cars and self-checkouts now, robots and machines yeah I know that one. Good word that, automation. Do you believe in God mate?

Me: Not really, I am Christian technically but I'm not that convinced by the arguments.

Gary: Well here's the thing. We are all inbred you see, right. Adam and Eve in the Garden of Eden. Well if they had kids, those kids would have to have mated with each other in order to make more kids, because they were the only ones. And I'm pretty sure that business with Noah ended the same way. You see a lot of people don't think about that. I see blokes going bald right, with beautiful Sheila's. You know the ones. They can be with the ugliest blokes, and they say no I love my husband even if he's bald. I say to them, you can't eat hair mate, but you can eat a T-bone steak. I'd rather have my teeth anyway. How many people have you got in the UK?

Me: I think it's over seventy million now.

Gary: Shit, and it's all free over there. Wow! seventy million. Tell you what, I heard that there are six billion Chinese people, that's crazy isn't it. Hey I've got this twenty-seven-year-old girl from America, pretty right. But I think she's having me on, you can't come over here I said to her. Did you have to do quarantine even if you are vaccinated?

Me: Yeah, I was double vaccinated before I came to Australia, and I still had to quarantine in Sydney, and in Brisbane eventually.

Gary: Fair dinkum. Well I better let you go cus I've got to make myself some lunch. What was your name again, Tom… Tom what… ah. I didn't look at your license because I didn't want to be cheeky. Hah! Hey have you got somebody at your new place to help you get the fridge installed?

Me: Yeah, I'll be fine it's not too heavy.

Gary: Hey you know anatomy books right. You can read one of those books and diagnose eighty per cent of your medical problems, because you know your own body don't you, doctor doesn't know. There was a bloke that I knew right who felt unwell all his life and it turned out it was a sinus problem. He had allergies that the doctor didn't diagnose, so I tell everybody now if they are sick check your sinuses it will make you better.

We shook hands, and so ended one of the most exceptional conversations that I have ever been a part of. I bet you wouldn't get that in Harvey Norman.

THE LADY IN RED

I was browsing through the aisles of Drake's supermarket one evening after work, when I walked past a red-haired lady with a guinea pig on her shoulder. I am not ashamed to admit that I followed her to the checkout to see what would happen. Quite nonchalant, the lady arrived at the till, where she realised that she would require two hands to pay for her items. So, she casually placed the guinea pig down on the counter in front of an inscrutable looking clerk, and then reached into her pocket for her purse. She opened the purse, paid for her shopping, put her purse back in her pocket, picked up the guinea pig which was now inspecting the chewing gum stacked next to the till, put it back on her shoulder, picked up her shopping, and left without the blink of an eye. That was a first for me at any rate.

TWADDLES

Twaddle's the clown is a patient of mine, although he normally prefers Ted as you might imagine. When I first met him, I called Ted into the clinic room and he sat down. I opened his notes to the reports section, and much to my surprise a picture of Ted, dressed as Twaddles, fell out. In my confusion, I extracted the photograph and saw that it had a message written on the back:

"If by chance someday you're not feeling well and you should remember some silly thing I've said or done, and it brings back a smile to your face or a chuckle to your heart, then my purpose as your clown has been fulfilled".

I've been an Audiologist for over ten years now, I can assure you that Twaddles is not something you see every day.

NICK

I had my tourist shoes on one weekend and was just on my way back from visiting the top of Mount Archer, when I stopped off at Rockhampton's famous Doblo Farmers Market. I was in my full UV protection gear that day, which included a hat with a 6-inch brim. The farmers market had closed unfortunately and the only signs of life were those coming from a cricket match, being played in the adjacent field, with the North Rockhampton Tigers. As I was returning to my car a voice rang out from the cricket field: *"oi longhorn"*. I spun around to see where the voice had come from. Just behind a tree were two men stood next to some white bleachers, one was wearing a cowboy hat and the other one had ginger hair and was wearing cricket pads. *"Oi, all right, want a drink?"* I looked over my shoulder to make sure that it was definitely me that they were talking to, and then pointed at myself with a quizzical look. *"Yeah you, come and have a drink".*

I walked over half expecting them to simply laugh in my face and send me on my way, after achieving the victory of getting me to walk over to them. On the contrary they earnestly shook my hand and the man with the cowboy hat produced a pineapple flavoured Bacardi Breezer; from the Esky that he had stacked against the bleachers. *"Why have you got gloves on"?* He asked me. *"Oh I've just been out walking and didn't want to burn the back of my hands"* I said. *"Righteo, well my name's Nick, hey what kind of hat is that?"* He asked. I told him and he got quite excited, *"yeah I used to have a hat like that".* At this point in the conversation Nick had picked up on my accent, and started jumping around a bit: *"hey he's a pom, I've got a pom here."* He then turned to the men sitting in the bleachers: *"I've got a pom here he's gonna beat the lot a ya's".* I am a disappointment to all my fellow countrymen but I have never actually played cricket, so I was pleased when Nick didn't ask me to take part in the game that was being played.

"I've never met a real pom before" Nick admitted *"I tell you what I hate is when they all say let's get mortal, you know that program they always show, Jersey Shore or whatever it is".* (Just so you know, Nick was colouring his pontifications with many more swear words than I have included here). *"Tottingham as well, Tottingham Hotspur, that's the best footie team I reckon, lost a lot of money on them".* *"Hey which team do you support?"* *"Bristol City"* I replied (also a lie, I don't follow the football either but that's the closest team to where I was born). *"Yeah, yeah"* said Nick *"know them... lost money on them too".* Nick went on to tell me how he used to be a rodeo rider, and that his cousin was good enough to ride in the professional circuit. Nick had suffered a life altering spinal injury several months earlier, and was no longer able to ride. He pulled up his shirt and showed me a big white Velcro brace that he now had to wear permanently, to keep his vertebrae in place. Without it he couldn't walk properly anymore. This was sobering because Nick can only have been in his 20's.

Nick went on to tell me that he wasn't playing cricket that day, he was just the energy, and I believed him. There was a moment in proceedings where I realised that even in a relatively isolated conservative town like Rocky, society was advancing. The men were all talking about the hot topics such as: pads that don't fit right, how the thickness of cricket bats makes a difference, how it's a pain that you can't have glass bottles on the green anymore, who the fastest bowlers were that they had each ever faced, you know the important stuff, when Nick suddenly broke off to shout abuse at a batsman who had mishit a delivery from his favourite bowler: *"hit it you fucking puf"*…but before he could finish putting emphasis on the final fricative, all the (much older) men sitting in the bleachers barked in unison: *'Oi'*, to cut him off. Nick apologised and they all went back to drinking. Humanity has a long way to go, as always, but I think that moment says a lot about how far we've come.

BRUCE

"Come on you pussy give it here", Bruce had said after witnessing one of his friends looking around for a bottle opener. Bruce was a Station Officer (SO) for the QLD Fire and Emergency Service. I met him at my squash club's Christmas party, and we got chatting over a slice of watermelon. He was a man who used the word *'righteo'*, as a verbal comma to punctuate his sentences with as he spoke. Bruce had joined the fire service in 1982 in Darwin, and he eventually moved on to Brisbane and then Rocky in that order. All firemen have to retire at the age of sixty-five, and he didn't have too long to go. A small part of him was looking forward to retirement because he had become jaded. He had given a lot in the line duty, and his injuries

136

now included a shattered knee caused by dismounting the fire truck on uneven ground, and several shattered vertebrae in his spine caused by a ladder falling on top of him. Quite the veteran, he had actually gone on to finish his shift that same day before seeking treatment.

Bruce had fought boat fires in Darwin, which were so hot, that the heat had actually caused the front of his helmet to melt. He told me that he couldn't understand the trend for all the latest generation of firefights, to want to look like strippers from the film Magic Mike. *"Those blokes fall over"* he told me. *"I once knew a world champion kickboxer, righteo, not an ounce of fat on him. After thirty minutes of fighting a fire you would see him start to go. He had nothing to lose you see. When you fight a fire you lose so much water that you come out lighter than when you went in, but he was already as light as he could be so he would just stop working. You'd have to pull him out"*. He went on to explain with a look of despondency: *"this new generation are all about being on Instagram or Facebook. They'll rock up at a car fire at the side of the road and take a selfie, to let the world know what they're doing. We all take the piss out of them but they've got thick skins"*.

Bruce educated me about all the generations of fire-retardant suits that he had seen come and go over the years, and that a lot of the research that fuels the development of new equipment comes out of the Fire Safety Engineering Faculty in the University of Edinburgh. One of the problems they faced with older generations of equipment was that many firefighters would end up with burns on the top of their head, as the heat would burn up through their trousers legs, travel through their insulated suits,

137

and scorch their scalps on the way out of the hood. *"Hey, why do firemen wear braces"* Bruce posed *"to keep their trousers up of course"*. He then proceeded to tell me about the alleged reason why the fireman's lift was replaced with the fireman's drag. The story goes that a fire once erupted in a Brisbane brothel.

When the fire brigade arrived to save the people trapped inside, they had used a ladder to enter through the top window to fireman's carry the ladies and their clients out to safety. Problem was, there was a solicitor on the street below observing the whole affair, who later encouraged said ladies to take out a lawsuit against the fire brigade for inappropriate sexual conduct. The fireman's carry as it was taught then required one arm to be passed through the legs of the person being rescued, to better balance them across the shoulders. The solicitor won the lawsuit and the fireman's drag was born; which involves dragging a person, by the shoulders or upper clothing, while they remain in a supine position across the ground. *"Then again"* said Bruce, *"when the time calls for it, you just have to do what you can"*.

We rounded off our conversation by Bruce telling me why he had become jaded during his time in the fire service. *"There are too many yes men becoming managers if you ask me, righteo. It used to be that SO's would work with their team in open plan offices, so that they could feel what was happening out there. But these new managers, they want to go back to the old way of sitting behind a closed office door, and giving orders from a distance. It's all right for them, this is their monkey house. When they swing across the canopy from the highest branches, they look down and all they see are smiling faces. When we look up, all we see are arseholes sat in high places."*

JOHN AND BOB

John owns a crocodile farm, and I met him briefly when I went out to take one of his family-run tours in Koorana. When I was there, I took some time to examine the extensive collection of crocodile artefacts, and newspaper clippings, which he had harvested from previous decades. They were all safely encased in glass cabinets around the museum restaurant. Amongst the collection was a laminated letter from a business owner called Bob, who had written to John back in 1983 with an investment proposal. Here is what the letter had said:

28.2.1983

Dear John,

It's not often one hears of a genuine opportunity for investment and perhaps you are not interested, but myself and some friends are participating in what I feel is a real boomer and not to be passed over. Simply, it is a cat farm. Initially we shall have one million cats. Each cat will produce twelve kittens per year so that after one year we shall have six million cats (females only produce!).

Now cat skins retail for fifty cents each for black and seventy-five cents each for white skins and presuming a fifty/fifty split, we shall have $3,750,000 worth of cat skins after one year. Now, a good Aboriginal cat skinner can skin fifty cats per day at a labour charge of only $15 per day, five days a week, and two hundred and fifty days a year or in other words, three hundred skinners for a cost of $1,125,000 will produce $3,750,000 worth of cat skins, thus giving a profit of $2,625,000 per year. We intend to establish the farm next door to your crocodile farm and this

139

would be your big chance to get rid of your skinned crocs. The cats will eat the crocs, one hundred cats eating 1 croc per day, and the crocs will be fed on the skinned cats.

So, the cats eat the crocs, the crocs eat the cats and we get the profit. Then we intend to open a snake farm adjacent and after more research, the snakes shall be crossed with the cats, thus producing a 'Snat', which will shed its skin twice a year, thus, eliminating the need for cat skinners, so even more profit. Should you be interested in this venture, send your application for shares with cheque to us as soon as possible and you won't regret it.

Yours Bob F.

Now, suffice to say that I was fascinated by this letter. Was it a joke? Was it genuine? If it was genuine who was Bob and what on earth did John say in response. If it was a joke, did it have the desired effect? My friends and family were split, my Dad was convinced that it was certainly a joke, my friend Connor thought it might be genuine. I had to find out, so I emailed John a few weeks after my visit to see what the story was behind this letter. The answer I got was well worth the enquiry:

0.12.2021
Hi Tom,

Bob was a lovable joker and a friend of ours back in the early 80's. He was an architect with a great sense of humour but drank too much. During one of his moments he penned the letter as a tongue in cheek investment opportunity. The letter gave us a good laugh but I was astounded how many people took it seriously. Cat lovers were not impressed.

It is just part of our history so we keep the letter on display.

I am pleased that you enjoyed your visit to Koorana so much. I have attached a pic of our largest croc as he died of old age last year. I caught him in 1986 and he was 4.8m long then. Measured out at 5.5m when hung beside my wife, Lillian.

Now that croc would need a lot of cats!

John

EPILOGUE

I arrived in Australia on the 22nd of March 2021. I settled when I arrived in Rockhampton in September 2021. It is now January 2022 and my heart has yet to flutter. I'm living a bit of an Australian stereotype: I'm eating kangaroo and barramundi weekly, I put Rosella jam on my toast, I've held a crocodile, I ate some crocodile, I drive a V6, I put chicken salt on my chips, I wear a palm leaf hat with a 6 inch brim, I drink my stubbys from a stubby holder, I skydived in Airlie Beach, I sun-burned the back of my hands whilst bushwalking, I watched the film The Castle, I grappled with a Huntsman Spider, I attended the professional rodeo surrounded by moustached men in Stetsons, I was set up on a date by a matchmaker at the local Catholic church, and I got to my feet out of respect for the national anthem. An interesting few months of saying yes essentially. Those who know me best have said that if anyone deserves to be here I do. But even if I choose to accept the premise that I had a special capacity to run harder and faster than anybody else, in the relay race that brought me to the lucky country, I know it would have meant nothing if all the people who assisted me hadn't put a baton in my hand to cross the finish line with. You can't win without that.

Regarding permanent residency and citizenship, it's too early to tell. My current VISA lasts me until October 2024, and I suppose it depends on just how many hoops I would have to jump through to make it happen. The rules keep changing, and the days of the Ten Pound Pom are over. I really get the sense that the system wants you to contribute as much as you can, take as little from it as possible during your time here, keep out of the cities, and then bugger off back where you came from. I'm certainly getting access to training opportunities that I couldn't get back home, here in the land down under. Nevertheless, looking forward to two and a half years from now, once I have acquired those skills through my service to the rural communities, it might well be that lucrative opportunities previously out of reach present themselves back in the UK, or elsewhere in the world. There are always friends and family back home to consider as well. I'm sensitive to the fact that it never used to be possible to count, using only two hands, how many times I could expect to revisit my nearest and dearest in person, across their lifespan, until I set foot on the other side of the world.

Permanent residency, or dual citizenship, would certainly be an asset in an ever more competitive global job market, if not for me than for hypothetical future generations of my family. But if it takes another gargantuan effort to make it happen come 2024, I will have to think very carefully about whether the juice is worth the squeeze.

And that's all I have to say about that.